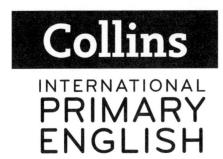

Collins
INTERNATIONAL PRIMARY ENGLISH

Teacher's Guide 4

William Collins' dream of knowledge for all began with the publication of his first book in 1819. A self-educated mill worker, he not only enriched millions of lives, but also founded a flourishing publishing house. Today, staying true to this spirit, Collins books are packed with inspiration, innovation and practical expertise. They place you at the centre of a world of possibility and give you exactly what you need to explore it.

Collins. Freedom to teach.

Published by Collins
An imprint of HarperCollins*Publishers*
The News Building
1 London Bridge Street
London SE1 9GF

1st Floor, Watermarque Building, Ringsend Road, Dublin 4, Ireland

Browse the complete Collins catalogue at
www.collins.co.uk

British Library Cataloguing-in-Publication Data
A catalogue record for this publication is available from the British Library.

Authors: Catherine Baker and Daphne Paizee
Series editor: Daphne Paizee
Publisher: Elaine Higgleton
Product developer: Natasha Paul
Project manager: Karen Williams
Development editor: Sonya Newland
Copyeditor: Karen Williams
Proofreader: Catherine Dakin
Cover designer: Gordon MacGilp
Printed and Bound in the UK using 100% Renewable Electricity at CPI Group (UK) Ltd

Cover illustrator: Richard Johnson
Internal designer and typesetter: Ken Vail Graphic Design Ltd.
Text permissions researcher: Rachel Thorne
Image permissions researcher: Alison Prior
Illustrators: Ken Vail Graphic Design Ltd., Advocate Art, Beehive Illustration and QBS Learning
Production controller: Lyndsey Rogers

Cambridge International copyright material in this publication is reproduced under licence and remains the intellectual property of Cambridge Assessment International Education.

Task sheets 1–3 and the Task sheet answers have been written by the authors. These may not fully reflect the approach of Cambridge Assessment International Education.

Third-party websites, publications and resources referred to in this publication have not been endorsed by Cambridge Assessment International Education.

With thanks to the following teachers and schools for reviewing materials in development: Amanda DuPratt, Shreyaa Dutta Gupta, Sharmila Majumdar, Sushmita Ray and Sukanya Singhal, Calcutta International School; Akash Raut, DSB International School, Mumbai; Melissa Brobst, International School of Budapest; Shalini Reddy, Manthan International School; Taman Rama Intercultural School.

MIX
Paper from
responsible sources
FSC™ C007454

This book is produced from independently certified FSC™ paper to ensure responsible forest management.

For more information visit: **www.harpercollins.co.uk/green**

Contents

Digital download with audio tracks available at
www.collins.co.uk/internationalresources

Introduction

About *Collins International Primary English*

Collins International Primary English is specifically written to meet fully the requirements of the Cambridge Primary English curriculum framework, and the material has been carefully developed to meet the needs of primary English learners and teachers in a range of international contexts.

The material at each level has been organised into nine units, each based around particular text types. The activities in each unit are introduced and explored in contexts related to the selected texts.

The course materials are supplemented and enhanced by a range of print and electronic resources, including photocopiable (printable) master sheets for support, extension and assessment of classroom-based activities (you can find these on pages 107–146 of this Teacher's Guide as well as on the digital resource). Reading texts are supported by audio-visual presentations.

Components of the course

For each of the Stages 1–6 as detailed in the Cambridge Primary English curriculum framework, we offer:

- a full colour, highly illustrated Student's Book with integral reading texts
- a write-in Workbook linked to the Student's Book
- this comprehensive Teacher's Guide with clear instructions for using the materials
- a downloadable digital package, which includes transcripts of the key texts on slideshows, audio files of readings, and printable PCMs.

Approach

The course is designed with learner-centred learning at its heart. Learners work through a range of contextualised reading, writing, speaking and listening activities with guidance and support from their teacher. Plenty of opportunity is provided for the learners to consolidate and apply what they have learned and to relate what they are learning both to other contexts and the environment in which they live.

Much of the learners' work is conducted in pairs or small groups in line with international best practice.

The tasks and activities are designed to be engaging for learners and to support teachers in their assessment of learner progress and achievement. Each set of lessons is planned to support clear learning objectives and the activities within each unit provide opportunities for oral and written feedback by the teacher, as well as self- and peer-assessment options.

Throughout the course, there is a wide variety of learning experiences on offer. The materials are organised so that they do not impose a rigid structure, but rather allow for a range of options linked to the learning objectives.

Weekly review

A weekly review section is built into the unit-by-unit teaching support in this Teacher's Guide. This review can be used for on-going assessment, as a tool to inform the next steps in teaching and learning.

Achievement levels are likely to vary from learner to learner. To provide support for differentiation, we have labelled the activities with either a square, circle or triangle.

The square, circle and triangle indicate what learners at varying levels might be expected to have achieved each week.

■ The square indicates what can be expected of almost all learners.

● The circle indicates what might be expected of most learners,

▲ The triangle indicates what level of achievement might be expected from learners who need a challenge.

A selection of follow-up activities is provided after each weekly review.

Cambridge Global Perspectives™

Cambridge Global Perspectives is a unique programme that helps learners develop outstanding transferable skills, including critical thinking, research and collaboration. The programme is available for learners aged 5–19, from Cambridge Primary through to Cambridge Advanced. For Cambridge Primary and Lower Secondary learners, the programme is made up of a series of Challenges covering a wide range of topics, using a personal, local and global perspective. The programme is available to Cambridge schools but participation in the programme is voluntary. However, whether or

Introduction

not your school is involved with the programme, the six skills it focuses on are relevant to all students in the modern world. These skills are: research, analysis, evaluation, reflection, collaboration and communication.

More information about the Cambridge Global Perspectives programme can be found on the Cambridge Assessment International Education website: www.cambridgeinternational.org/programmes-and-qualifications/cambridge-global-perspectives.

Collins supports Cambridge Global Perspectives by including activities, tasks and projects in our Cambridge Primary and Lower Secondary courses which develop and apply these skills. The content of the activities encourages practice and development of the Cambridge Global Perspectives skills to support teachers in integrating and embedding them into students' learning across all school subjects. Please note that the activities are not intended to correlate with the specific topics in the Challenges in the Cambridge Primary Global Perspectives curriculum framework.

Activities in this book that link to the Cambridge Global Perspectives are listed at the back of this book on page 147.

Teacher's Guide

The Teacher's Guide offers detailed guidance for covering each unit. Each unit is designed to cover three teaching weeks. The teacher knows their class and context best, so they should feel free to vary the pace and the amount of work covered each week to suit their circumstances. Each unit has a clear structure, with an introduction, suggestions for introducing the unit, lesson outcomes and a resource list of supporting materials that can be used in the unit.

Student's Book

The Student's Book offers a clear structure and easy-to-follow design to help learners to navigate the course. The following features are found at all levels:

- A range of fiction, non-fiction, poetry, playscripts and transactional texts are provided to use as a starting point for contextualised learning. Learners explore language through speaking and reading and then apply what they have discovered in writing. Notes provide a focus on different genres of texts.

- Clear instruction rubrics are provided for each activity. The rubrics allow learners to develop more and more independent learning as they begin to master and understand instructive text.
- All of the reading texts have audio-visual support available as downloadable files. Teachers can play these to the class and learners can use these themselves if they need to listen to the text again.
- Grammar and language boxes provide teaching text and examples to show the language feature in use. These are coloured so that learners can easily recognise them as they work through the course.
- The notepad feature contains reminders, hints and interesting facts.

Workbook

The Workbook is clearly linked to the Student's Book. The activities here contain structured spaces for learners to record answers. The activities can be used as classroom tasks, for homework, or for assessment purposes. The completed Workbook tasks give the teacher an opportunity to check work and give written feedback. Learners have a consolidated record of their work and parents or guardians can see what kind of activities learners are doing in class.

Digital resources

The digital resources are offered as a downloadable package. You can access these at www.collins.co.uk/internationalresources. These resources can be used to support learning and on-going assessment. The unit guidelines in this Teacher's Guide offer suggestions for when and how to use these resources.

All of the reading and listening texts in the course have been recorded and are supplied in the downloadable package as audio recordings. The audio recordings offer a range of voices, pace and expression and they will enhance the classroom experience by introducing variety and making it easier for the teacher to observe learners as they listen to, and follow texts.

We suggest that you use the audio recordings as you introduce each reading text. Learners can either listen only or follow the transcript provided on the slides or in their books as they listen to the text. Following and listening allows them to hear the

Introduction

words and the correct pronunciation and also to get a sense of where to pause, where to change expression and how to pace themselves when they are reading aloud.

Some materials can be printed out for use in the classroom. For example, there is an additional activity provided for each unit, with a supporting PCM. These tasks are teacher marked.

E-books

E-books are available for all components. The e-books can be used in a reader view on computer screens and are also designed to be used with interactive whiteboards and if available, iPads and tablets. Each e-book has standard functionality such as scrolling, zooming, an interactive Contents page and the ability to make notes and highlight sections digitally.

Assessment in Primary English

In the *Collins International Primary English* course, assessment is a continuous, planned process that involves collecting information about learner progress and learning in order to provide constructive feedback to both learners and parents or guardians and also to guide planning and the next teaching steps.

The Cambridge Primary English curriculum framework makes it clear what learners are expected to learn and achieve at each level. Our task as teachers is to assess whether or not the learners have achieved the stated goals using clearly focused, varied, reliable and flexible methods of assessment.

In the *Collins International Primary English* course, assessment is continuous and in-built. It applies the principles of international best practice and ensures that assessment:

- is ongoing and regular
- supports individual achievement and allows for learners to reflect on their learning and set targets for themselves
- provides feedback and encouragement to the learners
- allows for integration of assessment into the activities and classroom teaching by combining different assessment methods, including observations, questioning, self-assessment and informal tasks

- uses strategies that cater for a variety of learner needs in the classroom (language, physical, emotional and cultural), and acknowledges that the learners do not all need to be assessed at the same time, or in the same way
- allows for, and prepares learners for, more formal assessment including controlled activities and tasks. Learners should not be tested at all at Stages 1 and 2, and up to Stage 5, formative assessment is preferable to summative.

The *Collins International Primary English* course offers opportunities for consolidation and reinforcement in the form of task sheets that teachers can use to assess learners' knowledge and understanding. These task sheets assess the skills and competencies developed in a cumulative manner. In some cases, learners will use the same texts as context; in other cases; they will be expected to read and make sense of an unseen text and to answer a range of contextualised questions based on that.

At Stage 4, there is a short consolidation task at the end of units 3, 6 and 9 that the teacher can use as part of their on-going assessment.

Registered Cambridge International Schools benefit from high-quality programmes, assessments and a wide range of support so that teachers can effectively deliver Cambridge Primary.

The information in this section is based on the Cambridge Primary English curriculum framework from 2020. You should always refer to the appropriate curriculum framework document for the year of your students' tests to confirm the details and for more information. Visit www.cambridgeinternational.org/ primary to find out more.

Introduction

Learning objectives matching grid

The types of reading texts and the objectives covered in each unit are listed here by strand for easy reference.

These learning objectives are reproduced from the Cambridge Primary English curriculum framework from 2020.

This Cambridge International copyright material is reproduced under licence and remains the intellectual property of Cambridge Assessment International Education.

1 Stories of the past	
Texts: *Ragged Schools* (listening text, historical non-fiction) *Street Child* (historical fiction) *Ebenezer Grimes's Diary* (diary)	
Reading	**4Rw.01** Use effective strategies to read unfamiliar words accurately and confidently, including using phonic, morphological and grammatical knowledge, segmenting and contextual information. **4Rv.03** Identify and record interesting and significant words, and synonyms, from texts to inform own writing. [Stages 3 to 6] **4Rv.05** Explore and comment on how a writer's choice of words, including verbs, strengthens the impact on the reader, e.g. *rushed* instead of *went*. **4Rv.06** Explore and comment on how a writer's choice of words, including adjectives an adverbs, enhances the meaning (shades of meaning). **4Rg.02** Explore in texts, and understand, the use of commas and apostrophes. **4Rg.04** Explore in texts the use of different connectives in multi-clause sentences. **4Rg.05** Identify connectives in texts. **4Rg.09** Explore and understand how past, present and future verb forms are used in texts. **4Rs.04** Explore and recognise how ideas are organised in paragraphs and sections. **4Ri.01** Understand the difference between fiction and non-fiction texts and locate books by classification. [Stages 3 to 6] **4Ri.02** Read and explore a range of fiction genres, poems and playscripts, including identifying the contribution of any visual elements or multimedia. [Stages 3 to 6] **4Ri.04** Read and explore a range of non-fiction text types. [Stages 3 to 6] **4Ri.05** Identify, discuss and compare the purposes and features of different non-fiction text types, including how texts persuade the reader. **4Ri.06** Explore explicit meanings in a range of texts. [Stages 3 to 6] **4Ri.10** Predict what happens next in a story based on previous events in the story. **4Ri.11** Make inferences from texts, including about story settings and characters. **4Ri.14** Locate and use relevant information from a text to answer questions. **4Ri.15** Answer questions with some reference to single points in a text. [Stages 3 and 4] **4Ri.16** Recognise, compare and contrast the themes and features of texts. **4Ra.02** Express personal responses to texts, including linking characters, settings and events to personal experience. **4Ra.04** Comment on how fiction reflects the time or context in which it is set.
Writing	**4Ww.07** Generate spelling rules from spelling patterns, and test them. **4Ww.08** Use effective strategies, including segmenting, spelling rules, visual memory and mnemonics, to spell a range of unfamiliar regular and exception words correctly. **4Ww.09** Use paper-based and on-screen tools to find the correct spelling of words; keep and use spelling logs of misspelt words, and identify words that need to be learned. [Stages 3 to 6] **4Wv.02** Explore and use alternatives for overused words and phrases. **4Wv.03** Explore shades of meaning in adjectives and adverbs (e.g. *tepid*, *warm*, *hot*), and use them appropriately in own writing. **4Wv.04** Choose and use words (including verbs, e.g. *rushed* instead of *went*) to strengthen the impact of writing. **4Wv.06** Use own lists of interesting and significant words, dictionaries and thesauruses to extend the range of vocabulary used in written work. [Stages 3 to 6] **4Wg.01** Consistently use accurate end-of-sentence punctuation. **4Wg.02** Begin to use commas to make the meaning of sentences clearer. **4Wg.03** Use apostrophes for singular and plural possession. **4Wg.05** Write multi-clause sentences using a range of connectives. **4Wg.06** Use past, present and future verb forms accurately. **4Wg.07** Experiment with varying verb forms in texts, including in direct speech. **4Wg.08** Use the verb *to be* accurately, including subject-verb agreement for different verb forms. **4Ws.02** Use paragraphs and sections consistently to organise ideas. **4Ws.03** Use connectives to establish links between paragraphs, e.g. *if*, *although*. **4Wc.01** Develop creative writing in a range of different genres of fiction and types of poems. [Stages 3 to 6] **4Wc.02** Explore and use different ways of planning to inform writing for particular purposes.

	4Wc.04 Develop descriptions of settings and characters to capture the reader's imagination. **4Wc.08** Develop writing for a purpose using language and features appropriate for a range of text types. [Stages 3 to 6] **4Wc.09** Develop writing of a range of text types for a specified audience, using appropriate content and language. [Stages 3 to 6] **4Wc.10** Adopt a viewpoint in non-fiction writing that is appropriate for the purpose and audience. **4Wp.01** Write legibly, fluently and with increasing speed. **4Wp.02** Make short notes to record information from a text and use them to inform writing. **4Wp.04** Evaluate own and others' writing, suggesting improvements for sense, accuracy and content. [Stages 3 and 4]
Speaking and Listening	**4SLs.01** Listen and respond appropriately, including asking and answering questions to develop ideas. **4SLg.03** Extend a discussion by contributing relevant comments and questions. **4SLg.04** Take turns in a discussion, making links with what others have said. **4SLp.02** Read aloud with accuracy and fluency, showing awareness of punctuation.

2 Mars: the trip of a lifetime!

Texts:
Listening text: *Information about Mars* (non-fiction)
Visit Mars – for the trip of a lifetime! (non-fiction advertisement, persuasive)
Incredible Astronaut Ice cream (non-fiction advertisement, persuasive)
Don't send humans to Mars! (non-fiction, persuasive)

Reading	**4Rg.02** Explore in texts, and understand, the use of commas and apostrophes. **4Rg.03** Explore in texts, and understand, the standard layout and punctuation of direct speech. **4Rg.04** Explore in texts the use of different connectives in multi-clause sentences. **4Rg.05** Identify connectives in texts **4Rs.03** Explore and recognise how ideas are organised in paragraphs and sections. **4Rs.04** Explore and recognise how points are sequenced and linked to develop ideas within and between paragraphs. **4Ri.04** Read and explore a range of non-fiction text types. [Stages 3 to 6] **4Ri.05** Identify, discuss and compare the purposes and features of different non-fiction text types, including how texts persuade the reader. **4Ri.06** Explore explicit meanings in a range of texts. [Stages 3 to 6] **4Ri.07** Identify key words and phrases that establish the main points in a text. **4Ri.12** Begin to distinguish between fact and opinion in texts. [Stages 3 and 4] **4Ri.13** Skim to gain an overall sense of a text. **4Ri.14** Locate and use relevant information from a text to answer questions. **4Ri.15** Answer questions with some reference to single points in a text. [Stages 3 and 4] **4Ra.02** Express personal responses to texts, including linking characters, settings and events to personal experience.
Writing	**4Ww.03** Spell words with a range of common prefixes and suffixes, including *trans-, pre-, -ion, -ation* and *-ous*. **4Wg.01** Consistently use accurate end-of-sentence punctuation. **4Wg.02** Begin to use commas to make the meaning of sentences clearer. **4Wg.05** Write multi-clause sentences using a range of connectives. **4Wg.07** Experiment with varying verb forms in texts, including in direct speech. **4Ws.01** Develop a logical sequence of ideas, making relationships between them clear. **4Ws.02** Use paragraphs and sections consistently to organise ideas. **4Ws.03** Use connectives to establish links between paragraphs, e.g. *if, although*. **4Wc.02** Explore and use different ways of planning to inform writing for particular purposes. **4Wc.08** Develop writing for a purpose using language and features appropriate for a range of text types. [Stages 3 to 6] **4Wc.09** Develop writing of a range of text types for a specified audience, using appropriate content and language. [Stages 3 to 6] **4Wc.10** Adopt a viewpoint in non-fiction writing that is appropriate for the purpose and audience. **4Wp.02** Make short notes to record information from a text and use them to inform writing. **4Wp.03** Explore and use different ways of laying out and presenting texts to suit the purpose and audience (handwritten, printed and onscreen). [Stages 3 and 4] **4Wp.04** Evaluate own and others' writing, suggesting improvements for sense, accuracy and content. [Stages 3 and 4] **4Wp.05** Proofread for grammar, spelling and punctuation errors, and make corrections, including using on-screen tools. [Stages 3 to 6]
Speaking and Listening	**4SLm.01** Speak with accuracy and sometimes at length in a range of familiar contexts. **4SLm.03** Use vocabulary precisely to make the meaning clear. **4SLm.04** Use non-verbal communication techniques for different purposes. [Stages 3 and 4]

Introduction

	4SLm.05 Show awareness of an audience, e.g. by adapting language and tone to engage them. [Stages 3 and 4] **4SLs.01** Listen and respond appropriately, including asking and answering questions to develop ideas. **4SLg.02** Respond politely to another point of view with a personal point of view. [Stages 3 and 4] **4SLg.04** Take turns in a discussion, making links with what others have said. **4SLp.03** Adapt speech, gesture and movement to portray a character in drama. **4SLp.04** Plan and deliver a group presentation on a familiar subject, including to a wider audience. **4SLr.02** Comment on the ways that meaning can be expressed verbally and non-verbally in different contexts.

3 The power of the sea

Texts:
Windy Nights, Sea Haiku, Tanka (poems with simple imagery from different times)
Tsunami (non-fiction explanation)
How sand is made (non-fiction explanation)

Reading	**4Rw.02** Identify stressed and unstressed syllables in multi-syllabic words. **4Rv.02** Explore words with common roots and compare their meanings. **4Rv.03** Identify and record interesting and significant words, and synonyms, from texts to inform own writing. [Stages 3 to 6] **4Rv.05** Explore and comment on how a writer's choice of words, including verbs, strengthens the impact on the reader, e.g. *rushed* instead of *went*. **4Rv.06** Explore and comment on how a writer's choice of words, including adjectives and adverbs, enhances the meaning (shades of meaning). **4Rv.07** Identify and recognise meaning of figurative language in texts, including alliteration and similes, e.g. *as ... as ...* **4Rv.08** Comment on the impact of figurative language in texts, including alliteration and similes. **4Rg.01** Use knowledge of punctuation and grammar to read unfamiliar texts with understanding. **4Rg.07** Explore in texts examples of adverbs and adverbial phrases, including their purposes. **4Rg.08** Identify adverbs in texts. **4Rg.09** Explore and understand how past, present and future verb forms are used in texts. **4Rs.02** Explore and recognise the key features of text structure in a range of different fiction and non-fiction texts, including poems and playscripts. [Stages 3 to 6] **4Rs.03** Explore and recognise how ideas are organised in paragraphs and sections. **4Rs.04** Explore and recognise how points are sequenced and linked to develop ideas within and between paragraphs. **4Ri.01** Understand the difference between fiction and non-fiction texts and locate books by classification. [Stages 3 to 6] **4Ri.02** Read and explore a range of fiction genres, poems and playscripts, including identifying the contribution of any visual elements or multimedia. [Stages 3 to 6] **4Ri.04** Read and explore a range of non-fiction text types. [Stages 3 to 6] **4Ri.05** Identify, discuss and compare the purposes and features of different non-fiction text types, including how texts persuade the reader. **4Ri.06** Explore explicit meanings in a range of texts. [Stages 3 to 6] **4Ri.07** Identify key words and phrases that establish the main points in a text. **4Ri.09** Explore implicit meanings in a range of texts. [Stages 3 to 6] **4Ri.11** Make inferences from texts, including about story settings and characters. **4Ri.14** Locate and use relevant information from a text to answer questions. **4Ri.15** Answer questions with some reference to single points in a text. [Stages 3 and 4] **4Ri.16** Recognise, compare and contrast the themes and features of texts. **4Ra.01** Enjoy independent and shared reading of fiction genres, poems, playscripts and non-fiction texts. [Stages 3 to 6] **4Ra.02** Express personal responses to texts, including linking characters, settings and events to personal experience. **4Ra.03** Develop preferences about favourite books and share recommendations with others.
Writing	**4Ww.04** Explore and build words with related roots and meanings, e.g. *medical, medicine*; *sign, signal, signature*. **4Ww.09** Use paper-based and on-screen tools to find the correct spelling of words; keep and use spelling logs of misspelt words, and identify words that need to be learned. [Stages 3 to 6] **4Wv.01** Use specialised vocabulary accurately to match a familiar topic. [Stages 3 to 6] **4Wv.03** Explore shades of meaning in adjectives and adverbs (e.g. *tepid, warm, hot*), and use them appropriately in own writing. **4Wv.04** Choose and use words (including verbs, e.g. *rushed* instead of *went*) to strengthen the impact of writing. **4Wv.05** Use simple figurative language, including alliteration and similes. **4Wv.06** Use own lists of interesting and significant words, dictionaries and thesauruses to extend the range of vocabulary used in written work. [Stages 3 to 6]

Introduction

	4Wg.10 Use adverbs and adverbial phrases appropriately. **4Ws.01** Develop a logical sequence of ideas, making relationships between them clear. **4Ws.02** Use paragraphs and sections consistently to organise ideas. **4Ws.04** Use organisational features appropriate to the text type, e.g. bulleted and numbered lists. [Stages 3 to 6] **4Wc.01** Develop creative writing in a range of different genres of fiction and types of poems. [Stages 3 to 6] **4Wc.02** Explore and use different ways of planning to inform writing for particular purposes. **4Wc.08** Develop writing for a purpose using language and features appropriate for a range of text types. [Stages 3 to 6] **4Wp.04** Evaluate own and others' writing, suggesting improvements for sense, accuracy and content. [Stages 3 and 4] **4Wp.05** Proofread for grammar, spelling and punctuation errors, and make corrections, including using on-screen tools. [Stages 3 to 6]
Speaking and Listening	**4SLm.01** Speak with accuracy and sometimes at length in a range of familiar contexts. **4SLm.02** Sequence relevant information to aid the listener's understanding. **4SLm.03** Use vocabulary precisely to make the meaning clear. **4SLm.05** Show awareness of an audience, e.g. by adapting language and tone to engage them. [Stages 3 and 4] **4SLp.02** Read aloud with accuracy and fluency, showing awareness of punctuation. **4SLr.01** Begin to evaluate own and others' talk, including what went well and what could be improved next time. [Stages 3 and 4]

4 Other people, other places

Texts:
Listening text: *The Clever Farmer* (stories set in other cultures)
Abunuwasi's House (fiction, stories set in other cultures)
The Brave Baby (fiction, stories set in other cultures)

Reading	**4Rw.02** Identify stressed and unstressed syllables in multi-syllabic words. **4Rw.03** Extend the range of common words recognised on sight, including homophones and near-homophones. [Stages 2 to 4] **4Rv.08** Comment on the impact of figurative language in texts, including alliteration and similes. **4Rg.02** Explore in texts, and understand, the use of commas and apostrophes. **4Rg.03** Explore in texts, and understand, the standard layout and punctuation of direct speech. **4Rg.06** Explore in texts a range of examples of quantifiers, e.g. *either, neither, both*. **4Rg.09** Explore and understand how past, present and future verb forms are used in texts. **4Rs.01** Explore and describe the main stages in a text from introduction to conclusion. **4Rs.02** Explore and recognise the key features of text structure in a range of different fiction and non-fiction texts, including poems and playscripts. [Stages 3 to 6] **4Rs.03** Explore and recognise how ideas are organised in paragraphs and sections. **4Ri.02** Read and explore a range of fiction genres, poems and playscripts, including identifying the contribution of any visual elements or multimedia. [Stages 3 to 6] **4Ri.06** Explore explicit meanings in a range of texts. [Stages 3 to 6] **4Ri.08** Explain how settings and characters are developed, identifying key words and phrases from the story. **4Ri.09** Explore implicit meanings in a range of texts. [Stages 3 to 6] **4Ri.10** Predict what happens next in a story based on previous events in the story. **4Ri.11** Make inferences from texts, including about story settings and characters. **4Ri.14** Locate and use relevant information from a text to answer questions. **4Ra.01** Enjoy independent and shared reading of fiction genres, poems, playscripts and non-fiction texts. [Stages 3 to 6] **4Ra.02** Express personal responses to texts, including linking characters, settings and events to personal experience. **4Ra.04** Comment on how fiction reflects the time or context in which it is set.
Writing	**4Ww.03** Spell words with a range of common prefixes and suffixes, including *trans-, pre-, -ion, -ation* and *-ous*. **4Ww.04** Explore and build words with related roots and meanings, e.g. *medical, medicine; sign, signal, signature*. **4Ww.05** Spell common homophones correctly to match their grammatical purpose, including *they're, their, there*. **4Ww.07** Generate spelling rules from spelling patterns, and test them. **4Ww.08** Use effective strategies, including segmenting, spelling rules, visual memory and mnemonics, to spell a range of unfamiliar regular and exception words correctly. **4Ww.09** Use paper-based and on-screen tools to find the correct spelling of words; keep and use spelling logs of misspelt words, and identify words that need to be learned. [Stages 3 to 6] **4Wv.02** Explore and use alternatives for overused words and phrases. **4Wv.03** Explore shades of meaning in adjectives and adverbs (e.g. *tepid, warm, hot*), and use them appropriately in own writing. **4Wv.05** Use simple figurative language, including alliteration and similes. **4Wg.03** Use apostrophes for singular and plural possession.

Introduction

	4Wg.04 Begin to use other punctuation alongside speech marks to punctuate direct speech. **4Wg.06** Use past, present and future verb forms accurately. **4Wg.09** Use a range of quantifiers appropriately for the context, e.g. *either, neither, both*. **4Wg.10** Use adverbs and adverbial phrases appropriately. **4Wc.01** Develop creative writing in a range of different genres of fiction and types of poems. [Stages 3 to 6] **4Wc.02** Explore and use different ways of planning to inform writing for particular purposes. **4Wc.03** Write character profiles to inform story writing. **4Wc.04** Develop descriptions of settings and characters to capture the reader's imagination. **4Wc.05** Write alternative beginnings and endings for stories. **4Wc.06** Begin to express a viewpoint in fiction through a character's opinions about a setting or other characters. **4Wp.02** Make short notes to record information from a text and use them to inform writing.
Speaking and Listening	**4SLs.01** Listen and respond appropriately, including asking and answering questions to develop ideas. **4SLg.03** Extend a discussion by contributing relevant comments and questions. **4SLg.04** Take turns in a discussion, making links with what others have said. **4SLp.01** Read aloud with expression, adapting the pace and volume appropriate to the content. **4SLp.02** Read aloud with accuracy and fluency, showing awareness of punctuation. **4SLp.03** Adapt speech, gesture and movement to portray a character in drama. **4SLr.01** Begin to evaluate own and others' talk, including what went well and what could be improved next time. [Stages 3 and 4]

5 The only problem is ...

Texts:
The Youngest (poem)
Meeting Mr Faulkner (fiction, real-life story dealing with issues)
Eleven Years Old (poem from different culture)
The New Boy (fiction, real-life story dealing with issues)

Reading	**4Rv.01** Use context to suggest synonyms for unfamiliar words. **4Rv.05** Explore and comment on how a writer's choice of words, including verbs, strengthens the impact on the reader, e.g. *rushed* instead of *went*. **4Rg.08** Identify adverbs in texts. **4Rg.10** Explore in texts, and understand, subject-verb agreement. **4Rs.02** Explore and recognise the key features of text structure in a range of different fiction and non-fiction texts, including poems and playscripts. [Stages 3 to 6] **4Rs.03** Explore and recognise how ideas are organised in paragraphs and sections. **4Rs.04** Explore and recognise how points are sequenced and linked to develop ideas within and between paragraphs. **4Ri.02** Read and explore a range of fiction genres, poems and playscripts, including identifying the contribution of any visual elements or multimedia. [Stages 3 to 6] **4Ri.06** Explore explicit meanings in a range of texts. [Stages 3 to 6] **4Ri.08** Explain how settings and characters are developed, identifying key words and phrases from the story. **4Ri.09** Explore implicit meanings in a range of texts. [Stages 3 to 6] **4Ri.11** Make inferences from texts, including about story settings and characters. **4Ri.14** Locate and use relevant information from a text to answer questions. **4Ri.15** Answer questions with some reference to single points in a text. [Stages 3 and 4] **4Ri.16** Recognise, compare and contrast the themes and features of texts. **4Ri.17** Identify the viewpoint from which a story is told. **4Ra.01** Enjoy independent and shared reading of fiction genres, poems, playscripts and non-fiction texts. [Stages 3 to 6] **4Ra.02** Express personal responses to texts, including linking characters, settings and events to personal experience. **4Ra.03** Develop preferences about favourite books and share recommendations with others. **4Ra.04** Comment on how fiction reflects the time or context in which it is set.
Writing	**4Ww.01** Explore and use silent letters (e.g. *knife, lamb*) and different spellings of words with vowel phonemes (e.g. short vowel phonemes: *umbrella, young* and *love* ('o' before 'v'); long vowel phonemes after 'w': *want, war, water, word*). **4Ww.06** Spell words with common letter strings but different pronunciations, e.g. *tough, through, trough, plough*. **4Ww.08** Use effective strategies, including segmenting, spelling rules, visual memory and mnemonics, to spell a range of unfamiliar regular and exception words correctly. **4Wv.02** Explore and use alternatives for overused words and phrases. **4Wv.03** Explore shades of meaning in adjectives and adverbs (e.g. *tepid, warm, hot*), and use them appropriately in own writing. **4Wv.04** Choose and use words (including verbs, e.g. *rushed* instead of *went*) to strengthen the impact of writing. **4Wg.08** Use the verb *to be* accurately, including subject-verb agreement for different verb forms. **4Wg.10** Use adverbs and adverbial phrases appropriately.

Introduction

		4Ws.01 Develop a logical sequence of ideas, making relationships between them clear. **4Ws.02** Use paragraphs and sections consistently to organise ideas. **4Wc.01** Develop creative writing in a range of different genres of fiction and types of poems. [Stages 3 to 6] **4Wc.02** Explore and use different ways of planning to inform writing for particular purposes. **4Wc.05** Write alternative beginnings and endings for stories. **4Wc.06** Begin to express a viewpoint in fiction through a character's opinions about a setting or other characters. **4Wc.09** Develop writing of a range of text types for a specified audience, using appropriate content and language. [Stages 3 to 6] **4Wp.03** Explore and use different ways of laying out and presenting texts to suit the purpose and audience (handwritten, printed and onscreen). [Stages 3 and 4] **4Wp.04** Evaluate own and others' writing, suggesting improvements for sense, accuracy and content. [Stages 3 and 4]
Speaking and Listening		**4SLm.04** Use non-verbal communication techniques for different purposes. [Stages 3 and 4] **4SLg.01** Begin to take an assigned role within a group. [Stages 3 and 4] **4SLp.01** Read aloud with expression, adapting the pace and volume appropriate to the content. **4SLp.02** Read aloud with accuracy and fluency, showing awareness of punctuation. **4SLp.03** Adapt speech, gesture and movement to portray a character in drama. **4SLp.04** Plan and deliver a group presentation on a familiar subject, including to a wider audience.

6 Making the headlines

Texts:
Malala's award (non-fiction, newspaper report)
Mini Mars mission (non-fiction, newspaper report)
Fossil Hunt (non-fiction, magazine article)
Make your own fossil! (non-fiction, magazine article with instructions)

Reading	**4Rw.01** Use effective strategies to read unfamiliar words accurately and confidently, including using phonic, morphological and grammatical knowledge, segmenting and contextual information. **4Rw.02** Identify stressed and unstressed syllables in multi-syllabic words. **4Rv.03** Identify and record interesting and significant words, and synonyms, from texts to inform own writing. [Stages 3 to 6] **4Rv.05** Explore and comment on how a writer's choice of words, including verbs, strengthens the impact on the reader, e.g. *rushed* instead of *went*. **4Rv.07** Identify and recognise meaning of figurative language in texts, including alliteration and similes, e.g. *as … as …* **4Rv.08** Comment on the impact of figurative language in texts, including alliteration and similes. **4Rg.02** Explore in texts, and understand, the use of commas and apostrophes. **4Rg.04** Explore in texts the use of different connectives in multi-clause sentences. **4Rg.05** Identify connectives in texts. **4Rs.02** Explore and recognise the key features of text structure in a range of different fiction and non-fiction texts, including poems and playscripts. [Stages 3 to 6] **4Rs.03** Explore and recognise how ideas are organised in paragraphs and sections. **4Ri.04** Read and explore a range of non-fiction text types. [Stages 3 to 6] **4Ri.05** Identify, discuss and compare the purposes and features of different non-fiction text types, including how texts persuade the reader. **4Ri.06** Explore explicit meanings in a range of texts. [Stages 3 to 6] **4Ri.07** Identify key words and phrases that establish the main points in a text. **4Ri.09** Explore implicit meanings in a range of texts. [Stages 3 to 6] **4Ri.11** Make inferences from texts, including about story settings and characters. **4Ri.12** Begin to distinguish between fact and opinion in texts. [Stages 3 and 4] **4Ri.13** Skim to gain an overall sense of a text. **4Ri.14** Locate and use relevant information from a text to answer questions. **4Ri.15** Answer questions with some reference to single points in a text. [Stages 3 and 4] **4Ri.16** Recognise, compare and contrast the themes and features of texts. **4Ra.02** Express personal responses to texts, including linking characters, settings and events to personal experience.
Writing	**4Ww.01** Explore and use silent letters (e.g. *knife*, *lamb*) and different spellings of words with vowel phonemes (e.g. short vowel phonemes: *umbrella*, *young* and *love* ('o' before 'v'); long vowel phonemes after 'w': *want*, *war*, *water*, *word*). **4Ww.07** Generate spelling rules from spelling patterns, and test them. **4Ww.08** Use effective strategies, including segmenting, spelling rules, visual memory and mnemonics, to spell a range of unfamiliar regular and exception words correctly. **4Ww.09** Use paper-based and on-screen tools to find the correct spelling of words; keep and use spelling logs of misspelt words, and identify words that need to be learned. [Stages 3 to 6] **4Wg.01** Consistently use accurate end-of-sentence punctuation. **4Wg.02** Begin to use commas to make the meaning of sentences clearer.

Introduction

	4Wg.05 Write multi-clause sentences using a range of connectives. **4Wg.07** Experiment with varying verb forms in texts, including in direct speech. **4Ws.01** Develop a logical sequence of ideas, making relationships between them clear. **4Ws.02** Use paragraphs and sections consistently to organise ideas. **4Ws.03** Use connectives to establish links between paragraphs, e.g. *if, although.* **4Ws.04** Use organisational features appropriate to the text type, e.g. bulleted and numbered lists. [Stages 3 to 6] **4Wc.02** Explore and use different ways of planning to inform writing for particular purposes. **4Wc.08** Develop writing for a purpose using language and features appropriate for a range of text types. [Stages 3 to 6] **4Wc.09** Develop writing of a range of text types for a specified audience, using appropriate content and language. [Stages 3 to 6] **4Wc.10** Adopt a viewpoint in non-fiction writing that is appropriate for the purpose and audience. **4Wp.02** Make short notes to record information from a text and use them to inform writing. **4Wp.03** Explore and use different ways of laying out and presenting texts to suit the purpose and audience (handwritten, printed and onscreen). [Stages 3 and 4] **4Wp.04** Evaluate own and others' writing, suggesting improvements for sense, accuracy and content. [Stages 3 and 4] **4Wp.05** Proofread for grammar, spelling and punctuation errors, and make corrections, including using on-screen tools. [Stages 3 to 6]
Speaking and Listening	**4SLs.01** Listen and respond appropriately, including asking and answering questions to develop ideas. **4SLg.02** Respond politely to another point of view with a personal point of view. [Stages 3 and 4 **4SLg.03** Extend a discussion by contributing relevant comments and questions. **4SLg.04** Take turns in a discussion, making links with what others have said.

7 Inventions

Texts:
Encyclopedia of Inventions (non-fiction, reference)
A Good Idea (poem)
I'm bored with walking to school (poem)
How do zips work? (non-fiction, reference)
Velcro (non-fiction, reference)

Reading	**4Rv.01** Use context to suggest synonyms for unfamiliar words. **4Rv.02** Explore words with common roots and compare their meanings. **4Rv.04** Use as many initial letters as necessary to organise words in alphabetical order, and to locate words in dictionaries and glossaries. **4Rg.09** Explore and understand how past, present and future verb forms are used in texts. **4Rs.02** Explore and recognise the key features of text structure in a range of different fiction and non-fiction texts, including poems and playscripts. [Stages 3 to 6] **4Rs.03** Explore and recognise how ideas are organised in paragraphs and sections. **4Rs.04** Explore and recognise how points are sequenced and linked to develop ideas within and between paragraphs. **4Ri.01** Understand the difference between fiction and non-fiction texts and locate books by classification. [Stages 3 to 6] **4Ri.02** Read and explore a range of fiction genres, poems and playscripts, including identifying the contribution of any visual elements or multimedia. [Stages 3 to 6] **4Ri.04** Read and explore a range of non-fiction text types. [Stages 3 to 6] **4Ri.05** Identify, discuss and compare the purposes and features of different non-fiction text types, including how texts persuade the reader. **4Ri.06** Explore explicit meanings in a range of texts. [Stages 3 to 6] **4Ri.07** Identify key words and phrases that establish the main points in a text. **4Ri.09** Explore implicit meanings in a range of texts. [Stages 3 to 6] **4Ri.11** Make inferences from texts, including about story settings and characters. **4Ri.14** Locate and use relevant information from a text to answer questions. **4Ri.15** Answer questions with some reference to single points in a text. [Stages 3 and 4] **4Ri.16** Recognise, compare and contrast the themes and features of texts. **4Ra.02** Express personal responses to texts, including linking characters, settings and events to personal experience.
Writing	**4Ww.03** Spell words with a range of common prefixes and suffixes, including *trans-, pre-, -ion, -ation* and *-ous.* **4Ww.04** Explore and build words with related roots and meanings, e.g. *medical, medicine; sign, signal, signature.* **4Wv.01** Use specialised vocabulary accurately to match a familiar topic. [Stages 3 to 6] **4Wg.01** Consistently use accurate end-of-sentence punctuation. **4Wg.04** Begin to use other punctuation alongside speech marks to punctuate direct speech. **4Wg.05** Write multi-clause sentences using a range of connectives. **4Wg.06** Use past, present and future verb forms accurately.

Introduction

	4Ws.01 Develop a logical sequence of ideas, making relationships between them clear. 4Ws.02 Use paragraphs and sections consistently to organise ideas. 4Ws.03 Use connectives to establish links between paragraphs, e.g. *if, although*. 4Ws.04 Use organisational features appropriate to the text type, e.g. bulleted and numbered lists. [Stages 3 to 6] 4Wc.02 Explore and use different ways of planning to inform writing for particular purposes. 4Wc.08 Develop writing for a purpose using language and features appropriate for a range of text types. [Stages 3 to 6] 4Wc.09 Develop writing of a range of text types for a specified audience, using appropriate content and language. [Stages 3 to 6] 4Wc.10 Adopt a viewpoint in non-fiction writing that is appropriate for the purpose and audience. 4Wp.01 Write legibly, fluently and with increasing speed. 4Wp.02 Make short notes to record information from a text and use them to inform writing. 4Wp.04 Evaluate own and others' writing, suggesting improvements for sense, accuracy and content. [Stages 3 and 4] 4Wp.05 Proofread for grammar, spelling and punctuation errors, and make corrections, including using on-screen tools. [Stages 3 to 6]
Speaking and Listening	4SLm.01 Speak with accuracy and sometimes at length in a range of familiar contexts. 4SLm.02 Sequence relevant information to aid the listener's understanding. 4SLm.03 Use vocabulary precisely to make the meaning clear. 4SLm.05 Show awareness of an audience, e.g. by adapting language and tone to engage them. [Stages 3 and 4] 4SLs.01 Listen and respond appropriately, including asking and answering questions to develop ideas. 4SLg.02 Respond politely to another point of view with a personal point of view. [Stages 3 and 4] 4SLg.04 Take turns in a discussion, making links with what others have said.

8 Putting on a show

Texts:
Listening text: *Peter and the Wolf* (playscript)
Peter and the Wolf (playscript)
Zlata's Diary (diary, real-life story with dilemma and playscript of same story)

Reading	4Rv.01 Use context to suggest synonyms for unfamiliar words. 4Rv.03 Identify and record interesting and significant words, and synonyms, from texts to inform own writing. [Stages 3 to 6] 4Rv.04 Use as many initial letters as necessary to organise words in alphabetical order, and to locate words in dictionaries and glossaries. 4Rv.05 Explore and comment on how a writer's choice of words, including verbs, strengthens the impact on the reader, e.g. *rushed* instead of *went*. 4Rv.07 Identify and recognise meaning of figurative language in texts, including alliteration and similes, e.g. *as … as …* 4Rg.01 Use knowledge of punctuation and grammar to read unfamiliar texts with understanding. 4Rg.09 Explore and understand how past, present and future verb forms are used in texts. 4Rs.02 Explore and recognise the key features of text structure in a range of different fiction and non-fiction texts, including poems and playscripts. [Stages 3 to 6] 4Ri.01 Understand the difference between fiction and non-fiction texts and locate books by classification. [Stages 3 to 6] 4Ri.02 Read and explore a range of fiction genres, poems and playscripts, including identifying the contribution of any visual elements or multimedia. [Stages 3 to 6] 4Ri.03 Identify, discuss and compare different fiction genres and their typical characteristics. [Stages 3 to 6] 4Ri.04 Read and explore a range of non-fiction text types. [Stages 3 to 6] 4Ri.05 Identify, discuss and compare the purposes and features of different non-fiction text types, including how texts persuade the reader. 4Ri.06 Explore explicit meanings in a range of texts. [Stages 3 to 6] 4Ri.07 Identify key words and phrases that establish the main points in a text. 4Ri.08 Explain how settings and characters are developed, identifying key words and phrases from the story. 4Ri.09 Explore implicit meanings in a range of texts. [Stages 3 to 6] 4Ri.10 Predict what happens next in a story based on previous events in the story. 4Ri.11 Make inferences from texts, including about story settings and characters. 4Ri.16 Recognise, compare and contrast the themes and features of texts. 4Ra.01 Enjoy independent and shared reading of fiction genres, poems, playscripts and non-fiction texts. [Stages 3 to 6]
Writing	4Ww.02 Explore and use spelling patterns for pluralisation, including *-s, -es, -y/-ies* and *-f/-ves*. 4Ww.03 Spell words with a range of common prefixes and suffixes, including *trans-, pre-, -ion, -ation* and *-ous*. 4Ww.07 Generate spelling rules from spelling patterns, and test them.

Introduction

	4Ww.08 Use effective strategies, including segmenting, spelling rules, visual memory and mnemonics, to spell a range of unfamiliar regular and exception words correctly.
	4Wv.03 Explore shades of meaning in adjectives and adverbs (e.g. *tepid, warm, hot*), and use them appropriately in own writing.
	4Wv.06 Use own lists of interesting and significant words, dictionaries and thesauruses to extend the range of vocabulary used in written work. [Stages 3 to 6]
	4Wg.06 Use past, present and future verb forms accurately.
	4Wg.07 Experiment with varying verb forms in texts, including in direct speech.
	4Wc.01 Develop creative writing in a range of different genres of fiction and types of poems. [Stages 3 to 6]
	4Wc.02 Explore and use different ways of planning to inform writing for particular purposes.
	4Wc.03 Write character profiles to inform story writing.
	4Wc.06 Begin to express a viewpoint in fiction through a character's opinions about a setting or other characters.
	4Wc.07 Write a simple original playscript.
	4Wc.08 Develop writing for a purpose using language and features appropriate for a range of text types. [Stages 3 to 6]
	4Wp.02 Make short notes to record information from a text and use them to inform writing.
	4Wp.03 Explore and use different ways of laying out and presenting texts to suit the purpose and audience (handwritten, printed and onscreen). [Stages 3 and 4]
	4Wp.04 Evaluate own and others' writing, suggesting improvements for sense, accuracy and content. [Stages 3 and 4]
Speaking and Listening	**4SLm.04** Use non-verbal communication techniques for different purposes. [Stages 3 and 4]
	4SLm.05 Show awareness of an audience, e.g. by adapting language and tone to engage them. [Stages 3 and 4]
	4SLs.01 Listen and respond appropriately, including asking and answering questions to develop ideas.
	4SLg.01 Begin to take an assigned role within a group. [Stages 3 and 4]
	4SLg.03 Extend a discussion by contributing relevant comments and questions.
	4SLp.01 Read aloud with expression, adapting the pace and volume appropriate to the content.
	4SLp.03 Adapt speech, gesture and movement to portray a character in drama.
	4SLp.04 Plan and deliver a group presentation on a familiar subject, including to a wider audience.
	4SLr.01 Begin to evaluate own and others' talk, including what went well and what could be improved next time. [Stages 3 and 4]
	4SLr.02 Comment on the ways that meaning can be expressed verbally and non-verbally in different contexts.

9 Imaginary worlds

Texts:
Listening text:
Sheetal's First Landing (story set in fantasy world)
Sheetal's First Landing (story set in fantasy world)
The Last Dragon (poem)
Lost Magic (poem)

Reading	**4Rw.03** Extend the range of common words recognised on sight, including homophones and near-homophones. [Stages 2 to 4]
	4Rv.03 Identify and record interesting and significant words, and synonyms, from texts to inform own writing. [Stages 3 to 6]
	4Rv.06 Explore and comment on how a writer's choice of words, including adjectives and adverbs, enhances the meaning (shades of meaning).
	4Rv.07 Identify and recognise meaning of figurative language in texts, including alliteration and similes, e.g. *as ... as ...*
	4Rv.08 Comment on the impact of figurative language in texts, including alliteration and similes.
	4Rg.03 Explore in texts, and understand, the standard layout and punctuation of direct speech.
	4Rg.09 Explore and understand how past, present and future verb forms are used in texts.
	4Rs.01 Explore and describe the main stages in a text from introduction to conclusion.
	4Rs.02 Explore and recognise the key features of text structure in a range of different fiction and non-fiction texts, including poems and playscripts. [Stages 3 to 6]
	4Ri.02 Read and explore a range of fiction genres, poems and playscripts, including identifying the contribution of any visual elements or multimedia. [Stages 3 to 6]
	4Ri.03 Identify, discuss and compare different fiction genres and their typical characteristics. [Stages 3 to 6]
	4Ri.06 Explore explicit meanings in a range of texts. [Stages 3 to 6]
	4Ri.07 Identify key words and phrases that establish the main points in a text.
	4Ri.08 Explain how settings and characters are developed, identifying key words and phrases from the story.
	4Ri.09 Explore implicit meanings in a range of texts. [Stages 3 to 6]
	4Ri.10 Predict what happens next in a story based on previous events in the story.
	4Ri.11 Make inferences from texts, including about story settings and characters.
	4Ri.13 Skim to gain an overall sense of a text.
	4Ri.16 Recognise, compare and contrast the themes and features of texts.
	4Ri.17 Identify the viewpoint from which a story is told.

Introduction

	4Ra.01 Enjoy independent and shared reading of fiction genres, poems, playscripts and non-fiction texts. [Stages 3 to 6] **4Ra.02** Express personal responses to texts, including linking characters, settings and events to personal experience. **4Ra.03** Develop preferences about favourite books and share recommendations with others. **4Ra.04** Comment on how fiction reflects the time or context in which it is set.
Writing	**4Ww.01** Explore and use silent letters (e.g. _knife, lamb_) and different spellings of words with vowel phonemes (e.g. short vowel phonemes: _umbrella, young_ and _love_ ('o' before 'v'); long vowel phonemes after 'w': _want, war, water, word_). **4Ww.05** Spell common homophones correctly to match their grammatical purpose, including _they're, their, there_. **4Ww.06** Spell words with common letter strings but different pronunciations, e.g. _tough, through, trough, plough_. **4Ww.07** Generate spelling rules from spelling patterns, and test them. **4Ww.08** Use effective strategies, including segmenting, spelling rules, visual memory and mnemonics, to spell a range of unfamiliar regular and exception words correctly. **4Wv.01** Use specialised vocabulary accurately to match a familiar topic. [Stages 3 to 6] **4Wv.03** Explore shades of meaning in adjectives and adverbs (e.g. _tepid, warm, hot_), and use them appropriately in own writing. **4Wv.04** Choose and use words (including verbs, e.g. _rushed_ instead of _went_) to strengthen the impact of writing. **4Wv.05** Use simple figurative language, including alliteration and similes. **4Wv.06** Use own lists of interesting and significant words, dictionaries and thesauruses to extend the range of vocabulary used in written work. [Stages 3 to 6] **4Wg.04** Begin to use other punctuation alongside speech marks to punctuate direct speech. **4Wg.07** Experiment with varying verb forms in texts, including in direct speech. **4Wg.10** Use adverbs and adverbial phrases appropriately. **4Ws.04** Use organisational features appropriate to the text type, e.g. bulleted and numbered lists. [Stages 3 to 6] **4Wc.01** Develop creative writing in a range of different genres of fiction and types of poems. [Stages 3 to 6] **4Wc.02** Explore and use different ways of planning to inform writing for particular purposes. **4Wc.04** Develop descriptions of settings and characters to capture the reader's imagination. **4Wc.05** Write alternative beginnings and endings for stories. **4Wc.07** Write a simple original playscript. **4Wp.02** Make short notes to record information from a text and use them to inform writing. **4Wp.04** Evaluate own and others' writing, suggesting improvements for sense, accuracy and content. [Stages 3 and 4]
Speaking and Listening	**4SLs.01** Listen and respond appropriately, including asking and answering questions to develop ideas. **4SLg.01** Begin to take an assigned role within a group. [Stages 3 and 4] **4SLg.03** Extend a discussion by contributing relevant comments and questions. **4SLg.04** Take turns in a discussion, making links with what others have said. **4SLp.02** Read aloud with accuracy and fluency, showing awareness of punctuation. **4SLp.03** Adapt speech, gesture and movement to portray a character in drama.

Handwriting is not taught explicitly in this course although handwriting is implicitly covered in the activities and supporting notes in the Teacher's Guide. We recommend that teachers choose a structured and suitable course for teaching additional handwriting skills at Stage 4 level.

Unit 1 Stories of the past

Unit overview

In this unit, learners will read a historical story and a diary entry that gives additional information about the period in which the story is set. They will develop reading strategies to help them understand unfamiliar words and also to understand the context and time setting of stories. They will answer comprehension questions and practise using powerful verbs and adjectives. They will plan and write their own historical story, using background information from the unit.

Introducing the unit

Talk with the class about what life might have been like in your community 150 years ago. What differences might learners notice if they could time-travel back to about 1860 or 1870? Record learners' ideas on the whiteboard. Prompt them to think about changes in education in particular. For example, did most children go to school in 1860? What might they have done instead of going to school? Discuss whether learners think life would have been better or worse for children in their community 150 years ago.

Introduce the idea that, at that time, most children had no access to schooling, and many children had to work for a living. The texts in Unit 1 reflect life and education in Britain in the 1860s when education was only for those who could afford it.

Week 1

Key strands and substrands: Lesson outcomes

Reading

- Read a story and find answers to questions
- Recognise works of fiction
- Explore meanings and make inferences and predictions
- Comment on how a story reflects the time in which it is set
- Comment on an author's choice of words
- Explore the use of sentence punctuation, including apostrophes, in texts
- Record interesting words in a spelling log
- Use strategies to read unfamiliar words

Writing

- Use spelling logs to record words and spell them correctly
- Use patterns and strategies to spell words correctly
- Punctuate ends of sentences and use commas correctly

- Use the past, present and future forms of verbs, including 'to be' correctly
- Use interesting alternatives for the word 'said'
- Choose and use words to strengthen the impact of writing

Speaking and listening

- Take part in a discussion, asking and answering questions and making comments and links

Resources

- Student's Book pages 1–6
- Workbook pages 1–6
- Slideshows: *Ragged Schools*; *Street Child*
- Audio files: *Ragged Schools*; *Street Child*
- PCM 1: Punctuate the story
- Resource books or websites about life for children in Victorian Britain

---

Unit 1 • Stories of the past

Student's Book page 1

Listening and speaking

Explain to the class that they are going to listen to some information about the Ragged Schools which were set up in the 19th century to help poor children get an education.

Prompt learners to think about the advantages and disadvantages of Ragged Schools as they listen. Then play the recording, or read the text to the class. You may need to repeat the reading a second time.

---

1 Listening text

Over 150 years ago, many children in Britain didn't go to school. Often, this was because their families were poor, so the children had to work hard to earn money for their families to live on. Poor families couldn't send their children to school, because going to school was too expensive. Also, if a child was in school, they wouldn't be able to earn very much money. Then their family might have to go without essential things such as food and clothes.

'Ragged Schools' were set up to help the very poorest children to get an education. The schools got their name because the children who went there were so poor that they only had ragged clothes to wear.

Unlike most schools at that time, the Ragged Schools didn't charge any money. They taught children to read and write and do basic maths, and they also trained the children in some of the skills they would need in adult life. For example, children who went to Ragged Schools often learned about how to look after their money and make it go further. Many of the children were also taught the basic skills they would need to do a job. As well as educating children, many Ragged Schools gave them food to eat.

It wasn't always much fun being a pupil in a Ragged School. The teachers could be very strict, and children were often made to do boring tasks such as writing a sentence out 100 times. If they didn't pay attention or didn't learn their lessons quickly, children could be punished or hit by the teacher. But some teachers were much kinder and tried to look after the children well, and prepare them for life in the adult world.

---

2 Organise learners into pairs, and discuss paired work rules with them. Write the rules on the board.

Paired work rules

- Take turns to speak.
- Do not interrupt when the other person is speaking.
- Listen to the other person's point of view and respond politely.
- Ask each other questions to find out more about what you both think.
- Decide how you will report back to the class. Both of you need to contribute to this.

Remind the pairs to use the discussion prompt in the Student's Book. Give them about five minutes to discuss the advantages and disadvantages of attending a Ragged School, and then invite each pair to report their views back to the class. Encourage the other learners to listen to each pair carefully, ask appropriate questions and make constructive comments.

A range of responses are possible, but prompt learners to consider the following if necessary:

- Plus: Ragged Schools gave poor children an education which they couldn't otherwise afford, and this would help them to get better jobs and do better in adult life.
- Plus: Ragged Schools gave children food at a time when many poor children became ill or even died because of malnutrition.
- Plus: Ragged Schools were free, so in theory even the poorest children could afford to go.
- Minus: If poor children attended school instead of working, they couldn't earn so much money, and their family might suffer as a result.
- Minus: The schools could be boring, and sometimes there were tough physical punishments.

When all the pairs have reported back, review the range of opinion in the class. Did all the pairs agree? If not, you could have a vote to decide on the issue.

3 In their pairs or in larger groups, learners should look at the two pictures on page 1 of the Student's Book. Encourage them to discuss the questions together and record their answers.

Answers

3 Answers will vary, but could include:

a In the picture of the Ragged School, children are using various different types of equipment. It looks as though the boys and girls are being

---

Unit 1 • Stories of the past

taught separately. A teacher is holding up a poster or alphabet board. One teacher is sitting behind a desk at the back of the class on a raised platform.

b The children in the Ragged School are probably learning how to use equipment they will need in their jobs later on. They are learning the alphabet/how to read.

c The class in the Ragged School is much more active than that in the modern primary school. It is also quite crowded, and it looks as though it could be dangerous. In the modern primary school all the children are sitting at desks and they have books and paper in front of them, so it looks as if they will be learning to read and write. They are dressed smartly and look ready to learn.

d Both classes contain a lot of children, and the children are a similar age.

e Learners' own answers

Student's Book pages 2–3

Reading and writing

Explain to learners that this story is set in London, England in the 1860s. This was a period of great poverty for many people. Parts of London were very overcrowded and a lot of people were extremely poor. Many children were homeless and lived on the streets, most of them did not go to school.

1 Read the story with the class. You could read it aloud to the class first to help them understand the dialect used in the story.

Point out to learners that the character Jim uses a London dialect when he talks. In this dialect, the word 'ain't' can be used instead of 'have not', 'am not' or 'is not', and 'no' can be used instead of 'any'. After you have read the story aloud, look together at Jim's sentences using 'ain't', and translate them into standard English – for instance, 'Ain't got no friends' would be 'I haven't got any friends.'

2 Then let learners read the text silently. Based on the information they have just read, learners briefly discuss how Jim might feel about leaving the Ragged School. Ask them to say what they think might happen next.

After learners have finished reading, briefly recap the main strategies for reading unfamiliar words accurately and confidently, including:

- using phonics to sound out the individual sounds in a word and then blend the sounds together to read the word
- using morphology, for example, prefixes and suffixes – to help pin down the meaning of a word
- using knowledge of grammar to check whether a word makes sense and fits with the grammar of the sentence
- segmenting longer unknown words into syllables to help with reading them, using what they know about the context of a text to work out if a word fits the context and makes sense. Revisit these strategies as necessary for individual learners, in this and other reading sessions.

Move around the classroom while the reading is in progress, assisting where needed and reminding learners to read silently if necessary.

3 Learners should then discuss and write the answers to the comprehension questions in pairs.

Many of the questions are open, but even for more closed questions, always allow learners their own variations in the answers, as long as the sense of the answer is correct, and the language used is correct.

Answers

3 a We get clues that the story is set in the past from the characters' clothing in the pictures, the fact that there is an open log fire rather than central heating, and the mention of the workhouse.

b Learners may feel that Barnie is worried about the boys and wants to find out more.

c Jim is worried that Barnie might tell the police because if he did so, Jim and the other boys might end up in the workhouse.

d The advantages for Jim, if he takes Barnie to see the other boys, are that he will get some hot coffee and a safe place to sleep. Perhaps it will also help Jim himself and the other boys to have a safer and happier life. The disadvantages are that he doesn't yet know if he can trust Barnie not to tell the police, and perhaps the other boys will be angry with him.

e Accept any sensible answer that is in keeping with the text, and includes some reasons for the learner's view.

f This is fiction.

© HarperCollins*Publishers* 2021

Unit 1 • Stories of the past

Workbook page 1

Reading

1–2 Ask learners to do activities 1 and 2 in their Workbooks for homework, so you can see how well they have understood the passage and the character of Barnie. If necessary, explain beforehand how to fill in the speech bubble, using full sentences to describe Barnie's thoughts, and how to fill in the spider diagram using brief words and phrases.

Ask learners to research children's charities that operate in your local area.

Extension: Learners could work individually; they may choose to interview someone connected with their chosen charity, and they could choose their own format in which to report back their findings (a written report, computer presentation or oral presentation).

Support: Learners could work better in groups or pairs, and you could suggest a charity for them to research. If necessary, give them a sheet with headings to help them structure their notes, for example 'Name of charity', 'What the charity does', 'Why people should support the charity'. They could give a brief oral presentation of their findings, using their notes.

Student's Book page 4

Reading and writing

1 Revise the correct forms of the verb 'to have' and 'to be' before learners tackle this question, so that you can check they know the standard English versions of these verbs. Then introduce the dialect word 'ain't' and ask learners to locate it in the story text.

2 Ask learners to answer the questions, and then share their answers.

Thinking deeper

Talk to the class about how people in different places may use different words, for example, mobile phone/cell phone/hand phone. Talk also about how people may use different grammatical constructions in non-standard English, for example: 'Get off of the bus', 'The information what I need', 'I should of'. Ask learners to suggest some modern examples used in their own communities. Make sure that they understand that non-standard English is not wrong or inferior/superior in any way. However, standard English is expected in formal written texts, such as formal letters and official documents.

Then have learners complete the role-play. The English they use should say something about where they come from or where they live.

Extension: Ask learners why they think the writer uses dialect in the text. They may feel that the use of dialect makes Jim's language more vivid and allows us to picture him more clearly, but accept any sensible and well-reasoned answer.

Answers

2 a "I haven't got a mother."
   b "I haven't got a father."
   c "I am not telling you any lies."

Workbook page 2

Verbs

1–2 Follow up the Student's Book activity with verb questions 1, 2 and 3, which can be done as individual activities either for homework or in class.

Answers

1 Present: You **are**; We **are**; They **are**
   Past: I **was**; He **was**; They **were**
   Future: I **will be**; It **will be**; We **will be**

2 a Present: **I am** the fastest runner in my class.
   b Present: Amira **is** my sister's best friend.
   c Past: Dad **was** very good at maths when he **was** my age.
   d Past: Jon's favourite meal **was** chicken stir-fry.
   e Future: We **will be** at Grandma's house this weekend.
   f Future: Sahar says she **will be** an astronaut when she grows up.

3 Question 3 is open; look for grammatical and well-punctuated answers that make sense in the context.

Student's Book page 5

Using powerful verbs

1–2 Introduce the idea of powerful verbs by talking about the verb 'went' in sentences like 'He went down the road'. Can learners think of other verbs that could be used instead, to give a clearer picture of how the person moved? Discuss some alternatives, for example: 'charged', 'sprinted', 'tiptoed', 'thundered', 'sidled', 'crept', 'plodded', and so on.

Learners could do activity 1 as a class or paired activity. Activity 2 should be done individually, so you

Unit 1 • Stories of the past

have an opportunity to assess learners' vocabulary choices and grasp of grammar.

Learners could start their own lists of powerful verbs in their spelling log which they can refer to later in their own writing. You could also create these verbs as a classroom display. Encourage learners to add other word classes too, such as powerful and effective adverbs and adjectives.

Workbook page 3
Powerful verbs

1–2 Finish this section with activities 1 and 2, which learners can complete individually or in pairs, in class or for homework. The answers are open, but look for interesting vocabulary choices that fit with the sentence grammar and make sense in context.

Student's Book page 5
Punctuation

Have a quick punctuation quiz. Write the following punctuation marks on the whiteboard and invite learners to come up and write a sentence using each punctuation mark: . ? " " , ' Explain that the apostrophe shows possession.

Revise any of the punctuation marks that are not completely familiar. Recap on the uses of the comma that learners already know about, that is, to separate items in lists, and at the end of speech before a speech mark.

1–2 Complete question 1 as a whole class or in groups, and check that learners record the sentences accurately in their books.

3 Discuss the question with the class. Can any of the learners explain how commas are used in these sentences?

If necessary, introduce the idea of clauses (parts of a sentence that contain a verb) and point out how the sentence 'What if Barnie told the police about them, and sent all the boys to the workhouse?' contains two clauses which are separated by a comma. Discuss how the comma helps us to identify the two clauses and see how they go together to make meaning in the sentence. Without the comma, it might not be so clear which words go together.

Workbook pages 4–5
Punctuation

1–4 Ask learners to complete activities 1, 2 and 3 as paired or group activities, or for homework. Activity 2 revises use of capital letters and activity 3 revises use of commas in lists, direct speech and tag questions. Try to have them complete at least one activity individually so you can assess their understanding more easily. You may prefer to leave activity 4 until Week 2.

Student's Book page 6
Spelling and vocabulary

You could introduce this spelling work now, or cover it in weeks 2 and 3 if you prefer.

Encourage learners to add words they find tricky to spell here to their spelling log.

Ask learners to read the information about verbs with double consonants. Challenge them to close the book

Unit 1 • Stories of the past

and then tell a partner what they remember about the spelling rules covered.

Write a list of verbs on the whiteboard (for example: 'pat', 'grin', 'trot', 'work', 'help', 'cover', 'follow', 'peel', 'cook') and ask volunteers to follow the rules as they add *–ed* and *–ing* to each verb. Go over the rules again if necessary so that all learners understand them.

1–2 Learners can then complete activities 1 and 2 independently or in pairs.

Encourage learners to use a print or online dictionary to check any spellings they are not sure of, and add any misspelled words to their spelling log for future practice.

Answers

1 **a** Check learners' answers
   b hopping, sitting, swimming, pattering, waiting, digging, hooting
2 **a** Ahmed is <u>putting</u> his socks on.
   b I love <u>eating</u> pizza.
   c Leena <u>waited</u> a long time for her brother.
   d Miguel's new top <u>fitted</u> him perfectly.

Workbook page 6

Spelling and vocabulary

Set Workbook page 6 as homework.

Answers

1 **a** putting; **b** cleaned; **c** (correct) **d** sleeping;
   e (correct); **f** (correct); **g** finding; **h** (correct);
   i hopped; **j** (correct)

Hand out copies of PCM 1, which tests learners' knowledge of punctuation. Ask learners to correct the text individually.

Extension: Learners should find the missing commas between clauses, and the commas before closing quote marks, as well as the more straightforward end-of-sentence punctuation. They should also be able to write a brief paragraph that continues the action appropriately, with mostly correct punctuation.

Support: Learners may need help to identify the correct placement of commas and speech marks. They may struggle to write a continuation paragraph, but they should be able to write at least a sentence or two, which may not be correctly spelled and punctuated.

Answers for PCM 1

The correctly punctuated text is:

It was a freezing night on the streets of London, and Jim and his little sister, Martha, were trying to get to sleep. They only had a thin blanket, two old coats and a few sheets of newspaper to keep out the cold. Their stomachs were rumbling loudly, because they hadn't eaten a scrap of food since that morning.

"Are you asleep, Jim?" Martha asked. "I'm hungry!"

"I'm hungry too," muttered Jim. "But we've got no food left, so we'll just have to hope we can find some tomorrow."

Just then, the children heard a very unwelcome noise. A policeman was coming round the corner towards them.

"Hey!" he shouted. "What are you two doing here?"

The children looked at each other. It was too late to run! What could they do?

Weekly review

Use this rubric to assess learners' progress as they work through the activities this week. You can use the activities suggested beneath the table to follow up on your on-going assessment.

Level	Reading	Writing	Speaking and listening
■	May need help and support to fully understand a story set in an unfamiliar time and place.[1] May struggle to decode and understand unfamiliar words.	Needs support to think of powerful alternative verbs that can be used in place of weaker verbs. May not always use verbs accurately in writing.	Needs support to collaborate with others in an oral/aural task. May struggle to organise thoughts when reporting.

Unit 1 • Stories of the past

●	Usually reads accurately and fluently, and is beginning to use inference to help them understand stories set in other times and places. May need support to read and understand some unknown and unfamiliar words.	Can usually think of a more powerful alternative for a familiar verb when prompted. Normally use verbs accurately in their writing.	Demonstrates attentive listening, and often remembers to collaborate with others when working orally. Ideas may not always be clearly organised when reporting.
▲	Reads with accuracy, fluency and appropriate expression, often using inference to help them understand stories set in other times and places. Uses a range of strategies to help read and understand unfamiliar words, including checking meanings in a dictionary.	Can often think of more than one powerful alternative verb that could be used in place of a familiar verb. Almost always uses verbs accurately in own writing.[1]	Demonstrates attentive listening and collaborates effectively on oral/aural tasks. Ideas are usually clearly organised and easy to understand.

Reading[1] Read another extract or short story that is clearly set in the past or in another country and help the learners look for clues about where and when the story is set.

Writing[1] Let learners choose one or two of the new powerful verbs they have found and write a short poem about it or draw/paint a picture to show what it means.

Week 2

Key strands and substrands: Lesson outcomes

Reading

- Read and compare different features of non-fiction texts
- Understand how verbs are used in different tenses in texts
- Express a personal response to a text
- Explore adjectives and connectives in texts
- Identify connectives in texts

Writing

- Explore shades of meaning in adjectives
- Use apostrophes for singular and plural possession
- Use appropriate features, language and a viewpoint to write for a particular purpose
- Write sentences with connectives

Speaking and listening

- Read aloud in pairs, paying attention to punctuation

Resources

- Student's Book pages 7–10
- Workbook pages 5–7
- Slideshow: *Ebenezer Grimes's Diary*
- Audio file: *Ebenezer Grimes's Diary*
- PCM 2: Extract from a diary
- PCM 3: Diary entry
- Diaries for the learners to look at

Introduction

Bring in some diaries for learners to look at. These could be published diaries, such as *Zlata's Diary* by Zlata Filipovic, or perhaps a section of a real or made-up diary that you have kept yourself.

Give learners a chance to read some diary extracts, and talk about how diaries help us to find out what happened from the point of view of the person who

actually experienced it. Let learners have a go at writing a short diary entry for the previous day, or for a recent significant day in their lives. Read and share each other's diary entries.

Follow this up by looking, as a whole class, at some of the common features of diary entries, including the first-person narration (for example, 'I did', 'I went'), the use of present and future tenses as well

Unit 1 • Stories of the past

as past tense, the fact that diaries often include information about the writer's feelings and intentions, the fact that entries normally start with the date (and sometimes with 'Dear Diary'), and so on.

Let the learners read the notes about the features of diaries in the genre panel. You can also let students make a copy of the diary entry and then annotate it to show these features.

Student's Book pages 7–8

Reading: comprehension

Once you are sure that learners are familiar with the features and purpose of diary entries, introduce the diary entry in the Student's Book. Explain that this is a made-up diary, but it is based on real historical events. Circulate as learners read the diary aloud in their pairs.

Remind them to look at the punctuation as they read, as this will help them to read with meaning. Answer any questions they have about unfamiliar vocabulary or the meaning of the passage.

Learners then answer the comprehension questions in their pairs.

Read the notepad text and remind learners that types of text are classified in particular ways, including diaries. They learned about the Dewey classification system in Stage 3.

Answers

a Ebenezer Grimes, who lives in London.

b Date and 'Dear Diary' at the start, first-person narration and recount of events from the writer's perspective, details about how the writer felt and what he intends to do next, use of present and future tenses as well as past tense.

c Check learners' answers. Accept any past, present and future tense sentences from the passage.

d He opened a 'Ragged School' to educate them, and a 'Home for destitute boys' who had nowhere else to live.

e Definition in learners' own words, but they should work out that it means 'very poor and homeless'.

f Open question, but learners should realise that after Dr Barnardo turned John/Carrots away and he died, Dr Barnardo was very shocked and upset. The experience made him vow never to turn a needy child away again, so that he could avoid other children dying in the same way that John/Carrots had.

g Open question, but learners should realise that it had a strong effect on the writer – he intends to tell everyone about Dr Barnardo's work and raise money himself to support it.

h Open question – accept any reasoned comparison of the two texts that draws on the differences and similarities, and expresses a justifiable view based on text evidence.

i Open question – accept any accurate one-sentence summary, for example, 'Dr Barnardo does very important work with London street children and the writer wants to support him.'

Workbook page 5

Punctuation

If learners have not yet completed question 4, they could do these for homework or in class.

Learners could complete PCM 2 either now or later in the week.

Student's Book pages 9–10

Using adjectives and connectives

Write some sentences containing adjectives on the whiteboard, for example: 'I ate a delicious ice cream', 'Jared saw an enormous ship at the harbour', 'Bella's bedroom is very untidy'. Invite learners to come up and underline the adjectives, and circle the noun that goes with each. Rehearse the role of adjectives in describing nouns, if necessary. Then ask learners to think of some more adjectives, and see how long a list you can make together.

1–2 Ask learners to read the information on adjectives and to complete questions 1 and 2 either individually or in pairs.

Answers

1 Accept any choice of sentences or phrases containing adjectives.
2 **a** cold, freezing
  b huge, big
  c grown-up, elderly
  d unusual, extraordinary

Encourage learners to read the information on connectives on page 10 of the Student's Book. Prepare some cards or sheets of paper with the

Unit 1 • Stories of the past

following connectives: 'because', 'but', 'and', 'or', 'however', 'so', 'therefore'. Invite learners to choose a card at random, and in pairs think of a sentence that includes the given connective. They can write the sentences in their books or on the whiteboard. Shuffle the cards and have another go, so that each pair writes at least two or three sentences with different connectives.

3–4 Learners can then complete activities 3 and 4 on Student's Book page 10 in their pairs. The answers are open, but look for accurate identification of connectives, and well-constructed sentences.

Workbook page 7

Reading and writing

Learners could complete activity 1 for homework.

1–2 Learners could also attempt activity 2 at this point if you wish, or you could reserve this for the start of week 3 if you prefer.

> *Answers*
> **1** and, because, because, However, or, but

Weekly review

Use this rubric to assess learners' progress as they work through the activities this week. You can use the activities suggested beneath the table to follow up on your on-going assessment.

Level	Reading	Writing	Speaking and listening
■	May need help and prompting to identify features when reading diaries.[1]	Just beginning to identify and use adjectives, not always completely accurately. Can sometimes place adjectives in a hierarchy of scale from weakest to strongest.	Pays some attention to punctuation when reading aloud.[1]
●	Can identify several features when reading diaries and, when prompted, may comment on the reasons or effectiveness of the features.[2]	Can identify and use a range of adjectives in own writing, normally accurately. Can usually place familiar adjectives in a hierarchy of scale from weakest to strongest.	Pays attention to punctuation when reading aloud to make meaning clear.
▲	Understands and can identify features when reading diaries. Can explain why the features are used and how they are effective.[2]	Can identify and use adjectives confidently, including less familiar ones. Can place adjectives in a hierarchy of scale from weakest to strongest.	Clear attention to punctuation which makes meaning clear when reading aloud.

Reading[1] Ask learners to write a diary entry about a recent activity they did at school, or something interesting that has happened at home. Give them copies of PCM 3 to assist them with the format. Remind them to use what they have learned about diary features, and to include as many of these as possible in their work. Then let them work in pairs and read one another's entries. They can identify the diary features their partner has used.

Reading[2] Give learners copies of PCM 2 if they haven't already seen it. They read another diary entry and answer the questions.

Speaking and listening[1] Let learners read short passages aloud with your guidance. Remind them to pause for commas and full stops to help make sentence meanings clear.

Unit 1 • Stories of the past

Week 3

Key strands and substrands: Lesson outcomes

Reading

- Explore and recognise how ideas are organised in paragraphs and sections

Writing

- Use paragraphs and sections consistently to organise ideas
- Plan a story, including settings and characters

- Write sentences with more than one clause and connectives
- Write legibly, using notes from another text to inform the story
- Evaluate own and others' writing

Resources

- Student's Book pages 11–12
- Workbook page 8
- PCM 4: Notes for a historical story
- PCM 5: Paragraph plan for a story

Before learners tackle writing their own historical story, give them the opportunity to read or listen to another historical story (based on any historical period). You could give learners a choice from the historical stories you have available in class, or choose a book and read part of it to them. If any learners have historical stories at home, encourage them to bring these in to share with the class.

Workbook page 8

Reading and writing (continued)

3–4 While this preliminary work is happening, if learners have not already completed Workbook activities 3 and 4, they could do these for homework.

> ### Answers
> 3 Learners' own answers
> 4 **a** freezing; **b** ancient; **c** ravenous; **d** terrifying; **e** tiny

Student's Book pages 11–12

Writing

Step 1: planning

This piece of writing can be tackled as an end-of-unit review.

Learners can work in groups or pairs to do the preliminary activities 1 and 2.

Allow plenty of time for learners to think about these activities and record their notes. They can choose whether to write a story about Barnardo, based on information from the diary entry, or a different historical story.

Support: Help learners structure the note-taking and encourage them to discuss their ideas. PCM 4 can be used to help scaffold the note-taking for learners that struggle with this.

When all groups have prepared a basic outline of their story, look back together at the example story on Student's Book pages 2–3. Discuss how the writer has divided the story up into paragraphs that move the action on. Tell learners that they are going to use a paragraph plan to help them write their story.

Explain to learners they will need to think about how the paragraphs in their story will work. One idea is to have a first paragraph that sets the scene and introduces the characters; a second paragraph that introduces a problem or issue; a third paragraph that shows a setback on the way to solving the problem; a fourth paragraph that shows how the problem is resolved; and a final paragraph that rounds off the story.

Extension: If time allows, learners may choose to write a longer story, with more than one paragraph for each of the suggested stages. PCM 5 can be used to help the learners to plan their paragraphs.

Step 2: Redrafting and revising

Encourage learners to use the checklist to help them revise their own writing, before sharing it with their partner or group.

Step 3: Improving

Remind learners of the rules for commenting on other people's work, and write them on the whiteboard so learners can easily refer to them:

Unit 1 • Stories of the past

- Always think of at least one good thing to say about a piece of work.
- When you are suggesting things that the writer could improve, be polite and give helpful examples.
- Take turns to speak, and respect each other's point of view.

Allow time for learners to redraft and revise their stories. Circulate amongst the groups and offer help as necessary. Encourage learners to use their best handwriting in their final drafts, as these will be displayed. You may wish to read and mark the drafts before learners revise them, so you can get a sense of which areas of their work need most attention.

When all learners have had the opportunity to finish their stories, share them with the class. Choose some to read aloud (with the authors' permission) and display all the stories on a noticeboard for everyone to read. Encourage learners to illustrate their stories for display.

Thinking time

Allow time for learners to reflect on what they have learned about children in the past through reading stories and diary entries.

Weekly review

Use this rubric to assess learners' progress as they work through the activities this week. You can use the activities suggested beneath the table to follow up on your on-going assessment.

Level	Reading	Writing
■	May need support when reading other historical stories as a preliminary to planning their own. May need help to identify how paragraphs are used to move the story along.	Can write a short and simple historical text based on information they have read, with support if necessary.[1]
●	Can read independently with some confidence and accuracy, but may need support to understand how paragraphs are used to structure a story.[1]	Can write a simple historical text based on information they have researched, mostly with accurate grammar and spelling.
▲	Reads with accuracy and fluency, and with prompting can explain how paragraphs are used to structure a story.	Can write a more extended historical text with accuracy and fluency, researching to find useful ideas and following a clear paragraph plan. Work is mostly accurate in grammar and spelling.

Reading[1] Guide the learners and work through the plan using PCM 4 again.

Writing[1] Guide the learners and work through the paragraph plan using PCM 5 again.

Unit 2 Mars: the trip of a lifetime!

Unit overview

In this unit, learners will look at two different types of persuasive text: advertisements and persuasive arguments. They will answer comprehension questions and learn about the features of persuasive texts, including orders/commands to the reader, the use of fact and opinion, and the use of persuasive vocabulary including adjectives. They will extend their knowledge of commas and connectives, and using what they have learned in the unit, they will research, plan and write their own persuasive text.

Introducing the unit

Bring in a selection of age-appropriate magazines, ideally including some aimed at children, such as *Aquila*, *The Week Junior* or *National Geographic Kids* magazine (though you can also use natural history and wildlife magazines and newspaper supplements aimed at adults). Give learners the opportunity to look through the magazines, and ask them to find any parts that they feel are intended to persuade the reader to do or believe something. This could include advertisements, letters pages, editorials and also any article which asks the reader to take action.

Share what learners have found, and discuss how many of the articles and advertisements in magazines, newspapers and periodicals are intended to be persuasive. Why do learners think this is? Look at some of the language features that help to persuade the reader, for example appealing to the emotions and an emphasis on the benefits for the reader.

Explain that in Unit 2 learners will read some persuasive texts linked to space themes, specifically the planet Mars. Discuss what they already know about Mars, and share ideas. If possible, show learners some photographs of the planet, for example from the NASA website.

Week 1

Key strands and substrands: Lesson outcomes

Reading
- Read an advertisement and consider its features
- Skim a text to locate information and identify fact and opinion
- Express personal responses to text

Writing
- Make short notes to record information
- Use accurate punctuation and different verb forms
- Spell words with suffixes and prefixes correctly

Speaking and listening
- Take turns in discussion and respond politely
- Listen and respond, ask and answer questions
- Give a presentation, speaking accurately and using precise vocabulary

Resources
- Student's Book pages 13–18
- Workbook pages 9–12
- Slideshows: *Would you like to go to Mars?*; *Visit Mars – for the trip of a lifetime!*
- Audio files: *Would you like to go to Mars?*; *Visit Mars – for the trip of a lifetime!*
- PCM 6: Persuasive writing checklist
- A recording of *The Planets Suite* by Gustav Holst (optional)
- Resource books or websites about Mars, and about your local area

Unit 2 • Mars: the trip of a lifetime!

Student's Book page 13

Listening, speaking and writing

What do learners already know about the planet Mars? Share their ideas, and if possible show them some photographs of the planet, for example from the NASA website.

If the opportunity arises, you could also play them part of 'Mars' from *The Planets Suite* by Gustav Holst. Ask learners to listen to the music with their eyes shut, and then to create their own picture or description of the planet, based on the atmosphere and pictures suggested by the music, as well as their existing knowledge about Mars.

1 Explain to the class that they will be listening to an information text that has lots of facts about Mars. Ask them to write two headings: 'Good things about going to Mars' and 'Bad things about going to Mars'. Explain that, as they listen, you want them to make quick notes, arranging the facts that they hear under these two headings. You may need to demonstrate briefly how to do this. Then play the recording, or read the text to the class. Repeat the reading a second time to help learners collect all the relevant facts.

> **2 Listening text** (The listening text also appears in the Workbook, page 9.)
>
> Would you like to go to Mars? Here are some Martian facts to help you make up your mind!
> - Mars is Earth's next-door neighbour! Earth is the third planet from the Sun, and Mars is the fourth planet. But even though they are neighbours in the Solar System, Earth and Mars are still about 225 million kilometres apart. It would take roughly 260 days to get from Earth to Mars.
> - Mars is smaller, colder and drier than Earth. The average temperature on Mars is −62° C. That's 62 degrees below freezing, which is colder than Earth's Arctic Circle in the middle of winter!
> - Mars is often called the 'Red Planet' because of its red soil. The soil on Mars is red because it is rusty (it contains iron oxide).
> - Mars's rusty, dusty soil is very dry indeed. Sometimes there are enormous duststorms on Mars – big enough to cover the whole planet!
> - Even though the surface of Mars is so dry, scientists have discovered that there is lots of frozen water under the surface of the planet. This means that if people ever travelled to Mars, they might be able to get the water they need by extracting and melting the ice.
> - The air on Mars is mostly carbon dioxide, which is poisonous to humans – so any visitors would definitely need a spacesuit to survive!
> - There are lots of interesting things to see on Mars. The massive volcano called Olympus Mons is three times bigger than Everest – and it is probably the biggest volcano in the whole Solar System. There is also an enormous canyon on Mars that is nearly as long as the United States of America is wide! At night, you would see not one, but two moons rising in the sky.

3 Organise learners into pairs, and remind them about the rules for paired work, using the Remember box on page 13 and the extended information below:

> **Paired work rules**
> - Take turns to speak.
> - Do not interrupt when the other person is speaking.
> - Listen to the other person's point of view and respond politely.
> - Ask each other questions to find out more about what you both think.
> - Decide how you will report back to the class. Both of you need to contribute to this.
> - Use non-verbal communication, such as looking at the audience and smiling, as well as words.

Remind the pairs to use the discussion prompt in the Student's Book. Give them about five minutes to decide whether they are going to persuade others that it's a good thing or a bad thing to go on a trip to Mars, and to find their three best reasons. Then give them a further five minutes to think about how they can put their ideas most persuasively. Encourage them to make brief notes to remind them what they are going to say. Then ask each pair to make a short presentation to the class. You could have a vote at the end and allow learners some time to evaluate their own talks or those of other pairs.

You could use this opportunity to talk with the class about some of the features of persuasive language, based on examples from the presentations. For example, pick out good examples of emotive language and rhetorical questions, such as: 'Who wouldn't want to visit this fascinating and beautiful planet? Would *you* want to miss this opportunity of a lifetime?'

Unit 2 • Mars: the trip of a lifetime!

Workbook page 9

Reading

The listening text also appears in the Workbook, page 9. Learners could complete the Workbook questions as homework, or as a follow-up activity in class. The answers to the Workbook activity are open, but learners should be able to justify why they feel a particular fact is a good or bad reason to go to Mars. In their persuasive paragraphs, learners should be able to pick up on some of the examples of persuasive language which you reviewed in class.

Student's Book pages 14–16

Reading and writing

1 Learners look at the advertisement. Help them to understand the features of advertisements. Ask questions such as, 'Why do you think some of the words are in big letters or bold print?', 'Why are there exclamation marks?', 'Which words do you read first? Why?' After learners have read the advertisement, ask them to look for adjectives that make things seem exciting and attractive (to persuade the reader). For example: 'unforgettable', 'unmissable', 'unimaginable', 'amazing', 'unbeatable'.

2 Learners work individually, reading the text silently. Tell them to put up their hands if they find a word they don't know, and write these words, with their meanings, on the board.

Move around the classroom while the reading is in progress, assisting where necessary and reminding learners to read silently if necessary.

3 Learners could discuss and write answers to the comprehension questions in pairs, or you may prefer to do this activity as a whole-class group, in order to share thoughts and opinions more widely.

Many of the questions are open, but even for more closed questions, allow learners their own variations in the answers, as long as the sense of the answer and the language used are correct.

> ### Answers
> **3** **a** Olympus Mons is a massive volcano on Mars.
> **b** An open question; learners should give clear reasons for their views.
> **c** You would need a spacesuit to keep you warm, and to supply breathable air/oxygen.

> **d** An open question; learners should give clear reasons for their views.
> **e** An open question, but one possible answer would be 'Feel the <u>unimaginable, dangerous power</u> of a Martian duststorm!'
> **f** 'Hurry – don't lose your place on this unmissable trip!'
> **g** For example, 'Mars is very different from Earth, but don't worry – we'll transport you safely and make sure you're safe and happy during your visit!'
> **h** An open question, but learners may feel that the question at the start helps the reader to feel that the piece involves them.
> **i** An open question; look for complete sentences with correct punctuation.

Student's Book page 16

Reading and speaking

Learners could work in groups or pairs, finding one or two advertisements to analyse. Encourage them to annotate the advertisements to show some of the persuasive features. Then go through the advertisements as a group and see if you can find any more. You could give learners copies of PCM 6 to help with this activity. Learners can then compare advertisements if they have more than one and do a short presentation to the class about the key features of their advertisements.

Extension: Working in groups, learners could write their own advertisements for a made-up product or service of their choice.

Support: Working in groups, learners could write their own advertisements for a made-up product or service of their choice. They could use PCM 6 as a checklist to help with this.

Use the notepad feature in the Student's Book to help learners understand the difference between facts and opinions. As a whole class, think up some statements of fact and statements of opinion, and write them on the board in two separate lists.

Thinking deeper

Learners work in groups. They discuss what they would and would not put in an advertisement for a trip to Mars. You could give them a few questions to consider. For example:

Unit 2 • Mars: the trip of a lifetime!

- Some people might be afraid of making the journey. What could you say to make them feel safe?
- What is exciting about visiting another planet (for example: the scenery, wearing a space suit?) Should you mention this in the advertisement?
- Would people want to travel alone or with a guide? Should you mention this?

Workbook page 10

Reading

1–2 Learners could complete this in class or for homework.

> ### Answers
>
> 1 a O; b F; c F; d F; e O; f F; g O; h O; i F; j O
> 2 Learners' own answers

Student's Book page 17

Using exclamations

Remind learners about exclamations in advertisements by using the prompts in the Student's Book. Exclamations are written as orders (imperatives). Encourage learners to work in small groups to come up with two or three exclamations/orders of their own, and write them on the board. Use this as an opportunity to correct any misconceptions.

Learners can then complete the Student's Book activity individually or in their groups.

> ### Answers
>
> a <u>Come</u> with us for the experience of a lifetime!
> b <u>Take</u> your feet off the table! (or with final full stop)
> c <u>Go</u> to sleep at once! (or with final full stop)
> d <u>Shut</u> all the doors and windows. (or with final exclamation mark)
> e <u>Help</u> me find my mobile phone! (or with final full stop)
> f <u>Come</u> and <u>play</u> football with Rajiv, Emma and me. (Not all children may realise that 'play' is also imperative).

Workbook page 11

Persuasive language

1–2 Learners could attempt the related Workbook questions for homework, either now or later in the unit.

Recap the use of persuasive language with the learners. Explain that the sentences in the Workbook are all in the 'imperative form'. The imperative form tells the reader what to do; they are orders or give advice or warnings.

> ### Answers
>
> 1 a <u>Watch</u> the sunset from your bedroom in the hotel.
>   b <u>Race</u> across the red sand in a sand yacht.
>   c <u>Visit</u> Mars this year!
>   d <u>Don't miss</u> this opportunity to go on an amazing trip.
>   e <u>Feel</u> the unimaginable power of a Martian duststorm!
> 2 a Come and swim with us.
>   b Help Mum get dinner ready.
>   c Learn to cycle outside.
>   d Eat your fruit.
>   e Put on a spacesuit and visit Mars!

Bring in some newspapers, magazines and advertising leaflets, and ask learners to collect examples of statements, questions and orders. Give them a few sheets each and ask them to use different-coloured pens to highlight the different types of sentence.

Extension: Learners will be able to do this activity independently with a high level of accuracy. Ask them to choose one good example of each sentence type and use them to make a poster showing the features of each type, for example: command/imperative verb at the start of an order, question word or verb at the start of a sentence.

Support: You may need to model this activity for learners, who could work in pairs or groups. If some of the learners in the class make posters to show the relevant features of each sentence type, you could use these as a prompt for the activity.

Unit 2 • Mars: the trip of a lifetime!

Student's Book page 18

Spelling and vocabulary

Use the information box in the Student's Book to introduce the spelling rules for the prefixes *un–* and *trans–* and the suffixes *–able* and *–ous*. Then ask learners to attempt the questions.

Answers

a unforgettable, unexciting, unimaginable, unbeatable, unmissable

b unforgettable, unimaginable, unbeatable, unmissable

c transfer, transport, transparent; glorious, dangerous, courageous, delicious

d Open question: accept any sensible and correctly spelled sentences.

Workbook page 12

Spelling and vocabulary

1–3 Learners could attempt the Workbook questions for homework.

Answers

1 **a** unpleasant **b** unkind **c** unhappy **d** unseen **e** unused **f** uneaten. Sentences are learners' own.

2 **a** usable **b** believable **c** acceptable **d** regrettable **e** adorable **f** doable **g** fashionable **h** enjoyable

3 Answers are open.

Follow this by exploring some more prefixes (such as *mis–, in–, ex–*) and suffixes (such as *–ment, –ly, –ing*) with learners. For each prefix and suffix, start by finding some examples and write them on the board. Ask learners to arrange them according to spelling, for example, whether and how the root word changes when the prefix or suffix is added.

Can they work out the spelling rules in each instance? Make a class poster to remind them of the rules, and add to it as learners meet more prefixes and suffixes.

Weekly review

Use this rubric to assess learners' progress as they work through the activities this week. You can use the activities suggested beneath the table to follow up on your on-going assessment.

Level	Reading	Speaking and listening
■	Sometimes struggles to decode unfamiliar words and may need support to understand how a persuasive text manipulates the reader's emotions.	Needs support to present their ideas clearly and may struggle to identify persuasive language.[1]
●	Usually reads accurately and fluently, with some appropriate expression. Beginning to understand how persuasive texts manipulate the reader's emotions.	Can identify some persuasive language and explain it in a short presentation.
▲	Reads with accuracy, fluency and appropriate expression, and understands many of the ways in which persuasive texts manipulate the reader's emotions.[1]	Can organise ideas effectively and explain use of persuasive language. Presentation effective and clear.

Reading[1] Ask learners to collect some more examples of advertisements and persuasive writing. Let them choose two advertisements – one which they feel is effective and one which is less effective. Ask them to tell the class about the persuasive features of each advertisement and why they feel one works better than the other.

Speaking and listening[1] Choose another advertisement and assist the learners to annotate the persuasive language in the advertisement.

Unit 2 • Mars: the trip of a lifetime!

Week 2

Key strands and substrands: Lesson outcomes

Reading
- Read non-fiction texts and find key words to understand main points
- Explore meanings and find answers to questions
- Understand how ideas can be organised in sentences and paragraphs
- Find connectives in texts
- Understand commas in texts, including in direct speech
- Identify and discuss how texts persuade readers

Writing
- Use appropriate language and content to write persuasive texts
- Use connectives in sentences
- Use commas in sentences
- Use different verb forms
- Use features of persuasive texts

Speaking and listening
- Adapt speech to portray character
- Discuss how to express meaning verbally and non-verbally
- Use non-verbal communication techniques and show awareness of audience

Resources
- Student's Book pages 19–23
- Workbook pages 13–16
- PCM 7: Using commas
- Slideshows: *Astronaut Ice Cream*; *Don't send humans to Mars*; *Story extract*
- Audio files: *Astronaut Ice Cream*; *Don't send humans to Mars*; *Story extract*

Introduction

Ask learners to form pairs or small groups, and design a snack that astronauts could eat in space. Give each group a sheet of paper and ask them to sketch their snack design. They should annotate their design with labels and captions that show what their snack is like and why it would be suitable for space travel. When the groups have finished, share their work and ideas as a whole class. Which snack would work best in space? Which would be the tastiest? If the class could choose just one snack to make, which would they vote for?

Student's Book page 19

Reading

1 Introduce the 'astronaut ice cream' advertisement in the Student's Book. Circulate as learners read the advertisement aloud or silently in their groups, and answer any questions they have.

2 Learners then answer the comprehension questions in their groups.

Extension: Learners can be given the further task of including at least two questions, statements and orders in their advertisement. Look for correctly spelled and punctuated sentences with accurate use of grammar.

Support: Learners can follow the structure of the Astronaut Ice Cream advertisement for support. Give them copies of PCM 6 if necessary, reminding them about the features of persuasive writing.

Answers
2 a Because it's similar to the type of food astronauts eat in space.
b 'highly advanced', 'tasty'.
c It is harder and it doesn't melt.
d Accept any appropriate sentences quoted from the text.
e Open question – accept any advertisement texts that include some persuasive features and use language appropriately.

Workbook page 13

Sentence types

Learners could complete the Workbook questions on orders, questions and statements either in class or as homework.

Answers
a I like chocolate biscuits best. (S)
b Have you seen my football? (Q)
c Come here at once, Kieran! (O)

© HarperCollins*Publishers* 2021

Unit 2 • Mars: the trip of a lifetime!

d Why do you always eat the strawberry sweets first? (Q)

e We wanted to go to the beach with Sam and Mina because it was so hot. (S)

f Be careful, or you'll wake the baby! (O)

g Mum says it's bedtime now. (S) (or Mum says, "It's bedtime now.")

h Who is the fastest runner in the class? (Q)

I Shut the door! (O)

j The monster was taller than a block of flats. (S) (or end with !)

Student's Book page 20

Listening and speaking

1–3 You could introduce this activity by sharing learners' responses to the prompts as a whole class rather than in pairs, if you prefer. You may need to model the activity for some learners, or invite a more confident member of the class to demonstrate how to talk like a robot, to get the others started. Give pairs time to rehearse their scenes before bringing the class back together to enjoy the performances. Encourage the audience to give some constructive feedback to each pair, based on:

- how audible the performance was
- how well the performers conveyed the situation and the characters, including through movement and body language
- whether the performance told a good story.

Remind learners that when commenting on someone else's work, it's important always to make some positive comments as well as highlighting what could be improved.

If you wish, you could ask learners to write up their scenes in the form of a short story or playscript, either in class or as homework.

Student's Book page 21

Reading

Introduce the idea of persuasive argument texts using the prompt in the Student's Book. You could read the text and complete the comprehension questions as a whole class rather than in pairs or groups, if you prefer. Either way, allow time for learners to discuss the ideas in the text and decide whether they agree with the writer or not. Encourage them to give reasons for their views; you may need

to model this for them by stating your own view on the issue, with reasons.

Student's Book page 22

Comprehension

Learners answer the questions.

Answers

a because people love exploring – in space as well as on Earth; also because we can make scientific discoveries by going to Mars

b setting up a colony on the Moon, or developing space-based solar power

c because robots don't need food or many of the other supplies that humans need, and they don't need to be rescued if something goes wrong

d Reasons include: the distance between Mars and Earth, which means there is a delay in communication and therefore that it would be hard for people on Earth to help people on Mars in the event of an emergency; that whatever happened on the trip, the people on Mars would have to deal with it themselves; and that we don't know what the effect of prolonged space travel would be on the human body.

e Open question so accept learner's own wording: the main point of the first paragraph is that even though humans love to explore, the author thinks we should not send humans to Mars.

f Open question: look for headings that show the main point of each paragraph.

Student's Book pages 22–23

Using connectives

Use the information in the Student's Book to introduce or remind learners about connectives. Ask each pair of learners to choose a book and give them five minutes to see how many connectives they can find (keeping a list). Then bring the whole group back together to see how many connectives they have found. Are any of the connectives more common than the others?

1 Ask learners to answer the Student's Book questions on connectives. They could do this in their pairs or individually.

Answers

1 a Open question, but for example, three sentences with connectives that show the order of ideas are:

Unit 2 • Mars: the trip of a lifetime!

'Firstly, think about the cost.'

'Secondly, think about the safety issues.'

'Finally, there are many more effective things we could spend our money on.'

b Open question, but for example, two sentences with connectives that show how ideas are connected are:

'However, although the study of space is important, I believe that we should not be sending people to Mars.'

'It is far more expensive to send people to Mars than it is to send robots, <u>because</u> robots don't need food and water, and <u>if</u> something goes wrong they don't have to be rescued.'

c Accept any sentence with the connective 'and'.

d Accept any grammatical sentence using the connective 'but'.

Workbook page 14

Connectives

1–2 Learners could complete the Workbook questions on connectives for homework.

> #### Answers
> 1 **a** but; **b** because, but; **c** First, then; **d** and, but; **e** if; **f** because, and; **g** If, first, because
> 2 Accept any correctly structured sentences using the connectives 'first', 'next', 'then', 'because', 'however', 'also', 'if'.

Student's Book page 23

Using connectives (continued)

Ask learners to read the information on commas, and then discuss it as a whole class. If necessary, remind learners that a clause is a part of a sentence that contains a verb (so for example, 'I went to the shops' is a clause containing the verb 'went', but 'on Saturday' is not a clause, because it has no verb).

Why do learners think the sentences with commas might be easier to read? (Because the commas help to show where one clause ends and the next begins – without commas, the reader might not always notice the join between clauses and this could be confusing.) Challenge learners to find some more sentences which have commas between the clauses, and share the examples they find. Then ask learners to answer the Student's Book questions.

> #### Answers
> 2 **a** After I came home from school, I went straight upstairs, because I wanted to see Marvin, my pet gecko.
> **b** It was getting late, although the sun was still shining brightly, and I didn't realise that it was past my bedtime.
> **c** Running down the road, Maria wasn't looking where she was going, so she bumped into Mrs Martinez, who was chatting to her friend.

Workbook pages 15–16

Commas, connectives and tenses

Learners could tackle the Workbook questions on commas, connectives, tenses and comprehension either in class or for homework. You could use this as an opportunity to revise the differences between sentences using past, present and future verbs, if necessary.

> #### Answers
> **a** Jamelia fumbled in her backpack, and a shower of objects fell out: an apple core, a torch, a small folding magic wand, a half-eaten chocolate bar and a hair band.
> **b** Jamelia pointed to the sky behind her brother's head, and Josh spun round, his mouth open in amazement. Flapping slowly towards them, its leathery black wings stretched wide against the sky, was the most enormous dragon either of them had ever seen.
> "What a beauty," whispered Josh, as he looked towards the clump of trees where the dragon was landing.
> "We've got to get a picture of this, or no one will ever believe it!"
> Jamelia fumbled in her backpack, and a shower of objects fell out.
> However, there was no sign of Jamelia's phone, because she had left it behind on the bus!
> Jamelia looked up hopelessly, but Josh was already running across the field, and heading straight for the dragon.
> **c** Learners should circle the following connectives (in order from the start of the story): 'and', 'as', 'or', 'and', 'and', 'however', 'because', 'but', 'and'.
> **d** 'We've got to get a picture of this, or no one will ever believe it!'
> **e** Accept any past tense sentence from the story.

Unit 2 • Mars: the trip of a lifetime!

f Accept any present tense sentence from the story.

g a Salamander Black

h In the countryside, because the text says that the dragon landed by a clump of trees, and Josh ran across a field.

i The children have probably seen a dragon before, because they are more surprised at the size and beauty of it than amazed to have seen it at all! Also, Josh immediately identifies it as a particular type of dragon.

j his sister

k Josh seems to know a lot about dragons; Jamelia has a folding magic wand in her bag.

l Open question: accept any answer in keeping with the text.

Extension: Ask learners to complete PCM 7 so that you can assess their ability to use commas correctly in lists, in direct speech and to separate clauses.

Support: Ask learners to complete PCM 7. Some learners may need additional practice in using and identifying commas in these three situations. You could ask them to collect examples from their reading, and make a classroom display of examples of each type of comma use. Encourage them to refer to the display if they are not sure whether or how to use commas in a particular sentence.

Answers to PCM 7

1 a Jack's bike has blue handlebars, red mudguards, a black seat and a purple frame.
   b Ever since our first day at school, Jack, Emily, Chang, Noah and I have been best friends.
   c "I have four pets," said Noah, "and I like helping to look after them."
   d "My pets are a rabbit, a goldfish, a stick insect and a gerbil," said Noah.
   e Charlie zoomed down the stairs, ran out through the front door and rushed to the playground.
   f The monster's favourite foods were snail kebabs, wasp sandwiches, creepy crisps and jellyfish ice cream.
   g "Come and have your dinner at once," said Mum, "or it will get cold."

Weekly review

Use this rubric to assess learners' progress as they work through the activities this week. You can use the activities suggested beneath the table to follow up on your on-going assessment.

Level	Reading	Writing	Speaking and listening
■	May need support to follow the concepts in a persuasive argument text. May need help to identify persuasive language and comment on its effectiveness.[1]	Beginning to understand how to use commas and connectives, but needs support to remember when to use them.	May need support when improvising a short scene in role; may benefit from discussing ideas in advance and being shown how to use their voices and word choices to convey character.
●	Can read and understand a persuasive argument text and can often identify specific examples of persuasive language, commenting on effectiveness when prompted.	Can normally use commas and connectives with some accuracy. Beginning to understand that commas can be used in different ways for different purposes.	Can usually improvise a short and simple scene in role, sometimes needing help and support with preparation.[1]
▲	Can read and understand a persuasive argument text, identifying a range of different uses of persuasive language, and commenting on their effectiveness.	Understands some different ways of using commas for different purposes, and can use both commas and connectives effectively in their writing.	Can improvise a short scene in role, including using language and expression effectively to communicate character.

36

© HarperCollins*Publishers* 2021

Unit 2 • Mars: the trip of a lifetime!

Reading[1] Work with small groups of learners. Choose one or two advertisements that the learners haven't seen before. Prompt them with questions to look for persuasive language in the advertisements.

Speaking and listening[1] Work with small groups. Give learners another scenario related to space travel. Let learners as a group suggest the gestures and movement the characters would make. Remind them that they may not be human, or they may be wearing heavy clothing which will affect the gestures. Ask them to think about how they would communicate. Ask them what they would say to each other. Then let learners work in pairs and improvise a short scene, using the ideas from the group discussion.

Week 3

Key strands and substrands: Lesson outcomes

Writing

- Plan writing in different ways
- Write in paragraphs, using a logical sequence of ideas
- Use appropriate language, contents, viewpoint and features of persuasive texts
- Consider different ways of presenting work
- Evaluate and proofread own and others' writing

Resources

- Student's Book pages 24–25

Student's Book pages 24–25

Writing

Before learners begin to write their own persuasive text, reread the Mars advertisement on pages 14–15 of the Student's Book. Explain that they will be writing their own persuasive text, giving reasons why readers should visit their own local area (or another place they know and like). Ask the group to think about good places to visit locally, or other places they have enjoyed visiting. Share their ideas for different places they could focus on in their texts.

Step 1: Planning

Ask learners to follow the prompts in the Student's Book as they plan their piece of writing. They could work in groups, in pairs or individually. It may help to divide learners up into pairs or groups depending on the places they have chosen to focus on.

Allow time for research – for those learners who are concentrating on the local area, you could bring in some information leaflets about local attractions and places to visit. You may also be able to arrange some visits from people involved in these attractions. Learners who have chosen to focus on another area could use books or the internet to find out information. Remind them to focus on things that would make a reader want to visit their location, rather than just general facts about the area.

If necessary, once learners have done their preliminary research and thinking, model how to divide the ideas and information they have found into paragraph sections. Each paragraph section should focus on a particular theme, as suggested in the Student's Book. Show learners how to create a paragraph plan by giving each paragraph a heading, and recording relevant facts and information under each heading.

Spend some time discussing the best layout for this work. Should it be handwritten or would it be best done on a computer? Why? What are the advantages and disadvantages of each?

Step 2: Redrafting and revising

PCM 6 can be used as a checklist to remind learners of the key elements they need to include in their persuasive texts.

Give learners the opportunity to write a full draft of their piece. You could choose to review the pieces at draft stage so that you have the opportunity to give learners pointers for improving their work.

Encourage learners to check their spellings and grammar carefully. If they are writing on the computer, remind them to use the available spelling and grammar checkers in the software they are using.

Extension: Learners may be able to structure their work as a persuasive argument text, giving reasons for their views about why their chosen place is a good one to visit. These learners should be able to write their pieces independently, even if they worked in a pair or group during the research phase.

Support: Work with learners to help them structure their work. They could write a relatively brief advertisement rather than a persuasive argument text, if you prefer.

Encourage learners to use the checklist on page 12 of the Student's Book to help them revise their own writing, before sharing it with their partner or group. Remind learners of the rules for commenting on other people's work, and write them on the whiteboard so learners can easily refer to them:

- Always think of at least one good thing to say about a piece of work.
- When you are suggesting things that the writer could improve, be polite and give helpful examples.

- Take it in turns to speak, and respect each other's point of view.

Allow time for learners to redraft and revise their writing. Circulate among the groups and offer help as necessary. Remind learners to take care with the presentation of their pieces and to include headings, bold text and illustrations to help persuade the reader.

Share all the advertisements and persuasive arguments with the class, and display them on a noticeboard for everyone to read. If appropriate, you could take a vote on which place sounds the most interesting to visit, based on the persuasive texts.

Thinking time

This activity can be undertaken as an end of unit review. Encourage learners to review all the advertisements and assess how each one uses the features of persuasive texts.

Weekly review

Use this rubric to assess learners' progress as they work through the activities this week. You can use the activities suggested beneath the table to follow up on your on-going assessment.

Level	Writing	Speaking and listening
■	Can write a short and simple persuasive text based on straightforward research, with support if necessary.[1]	Needs support to articulate their thoughts when discussing writing ideas, or commenting on others' writing.[1]
●	Can write a simple persuasive text based on research, mostly with accurate grammar and spelling.	Can normally contribute appropriately (though sometimes briefly) to a discussion of writing ideas. Normally listens to and comments on others' writing courteously.
▲	Can write a more extended persuasive text with accuracy and fluency, adding their own ideas to information they have read.	Contributes independently and appropriately to discussions of writing ideas, and can make helpful suggestions for improvement when reviewing others' writing.

Writing[1] Pair learners who have written about the same local place. Let them compare what they have written and decide what works well and what could be improved. Let them choose the best ideas from each piece of writing and combine it into one text. You can prompt them as well about what they could add or improve.

Speaking and listening[1] Some learners may feel shy or may not want to be seen to criticise the work of others. Work through point 6 of the Writing activity with them in small groups again and help them to find kind words in which to express their ideas about the work of others.

Unit 3 The power of the sea

Unit overview

In this unit, learners will read a range of poetry from different times and cultures on the theme of the sea, including haiku and tanka. They will also read some non-fiction texts related to the sea, and answer comprehension questions. Learners will also consider how each type of text uses language effectively, and write their own poems and explanation texts based on models in the Student's Book. They will learn more about powerful verbs, adverbs and adjectives, and explore spellings in the context of word families.

Introducing the unit

Elicit learners' experiences of the sea. These are likely to vary depending on how close to the sea they live. Show some suitable video clips of the sea in calm and stormy weather. Explain that the sea has always been a source of inspiration for art, including poetry. Why do learners think this might be? Tell learners that poets have tried to capture the different moods of the sea in many different ways and in different poetic forms, from rhyming and rhythmic poetry to short verse forms like haiku and tanka, to free verse. Explain that in Unit 3 they will read and respond to a variety of different poems on the theme of the sea.

If you have musical instruments available and it is appropriate, use them to create sounds of the sea with the learners. Then ask learners to suggest words to describe the sounds you have created.

Week 1

Key strands and substrands: Lesson outcomes

Reading

- Read poems in pairs and give personal responses
- Comment on writer's choice of words
- Understand meanings in and make inference from texts
- Identify, understand and comment on similes
- Identify stressed and unstressed syllables in words
- Use punctuation and grammar to understand unfamiliar texts
- Compare themes and features of texts
- Share and recommend poetry

Writing

- Use specialised vocabulary and choose words with impact
- Use similes in own writing
- Record words in a spelling log
- Explore meaning in adverbs and adjectives

- Plan writing and proofread afterwards
- Develop creative writing skills by writing simple poetry

Speaking and listening

- Use precise vocabulary
- Read aloud fluently with appropriate expression and pace

Resources

- Student's Book pages 26–30
- Workbook pages 17–18
- Slideshows: *Windy Nights*; *Sea Haiku*; *Tanka*; *Old Man Ocean*
- Audio files: *Windy Nights*; *Sea Haiku*; *Tanka*; *Old Man Ocean*
- PCM 8: Descriptive words and phrases
- Source an audio recording of *Hebrides Overture: Fingal's Cave* by Felix Mendelssohn
- Video clips of the ocean

Student's Book page 26

Speaking and writing

Groups that are very familiar with the sea should be able to talk about what it's like in different weathers, different times of day or times of year, and how it makes them feel. Groups that have less experience of the sea can be asked to imagine what it might be like to live near the sea, and share their experiences of visiting it.

Write a quick list of the advantages and disadvantages of living near the sea, recording learners' ideas.

© HarperCollins*Publishers* 2021

Unit 3 • The power of the sea

Explain to learners that they are going to look at some photographs of the sea and listen to a piece of music composed with the sea in mind.

Tell learners that in 1829 a German composer called Felix Mendelssohn visited the Scottish island of Staffa. On this island is a very special cave by the sea, called Fingal's Cave, which is over 60 metres deep. When the sea is stormy, the waves roar and rumble inside the cave, creating some very loud, atmospheric sounds. Mendelssohn was so inspired by his visit to Staffa that he wrote this piece of music about the cave.

Explain that you would like learners to look at the photographs as they listen to the music, and think about what it would be like to be standing by the sea. Ask them to use the bullet-point prompts on page 26 of the Student's Book to help them make some quick notes as they listen (or give them copies of PCM 8 to fill in).

Play the music at least twice to allow learners to record their thoughts, and then ask them to form pairs to discuss and improve their words and phrases. When learners have had a chance to do this, bring the class back together and make a list of the most descriptive phrases that the pairs have come up with.

Student's Book pages 27–28

Reading and writing

1 Read the poems aloud to the class. Try to emphasis the rhythm and mood of each poem as you do this.

Explain alliteration and read some examples from the poems aloud again to emphasise how this helps to give a poem rhythm.

Revise similes and give some examples with 'as ... as' and 'like'.

Learners work in pairs, taking turns to read the poems out loud to their partners. Allow the pairs a few minutes to discuss the poems, and circulate as they do this so that you can help if any of the pairs have difficulties.

Bring the whole class back together briefly to talk about the poems and their initial responses. Ask individuals to tell the group which poem they liked best, and why. If any learners are unsure of the meanings of any of the poems, or if they are puzzled by any of the words, help them to understand. Write any unfamiliar words on the board, with their definitions.

2 Discuss the questions as a whole-class group. Many of the questions are open but learners may need help to express their answers. Allow learners their own

variations as long as the sense of the answer is correct.

You may ask learners to work in pairs and write their answers to the questions after the whole-group discussion.

Working in small groups, learners can then choose one of the poems and practise reciting it with appropriate expression. You could share their readings in class or in an assembly or performance for parents.

Answers

2 a Any accurate description in the learner's own words. They should pick up that the setting is near the sea, in the countryside, by a road, on a stormy night.

b set/wet, high/by, out/about

c This is an open question, but learners should pick up that the noise is probably made by the wind in the trees.

d Accept any answer that makes sense in the context of the poem.

e The simile is 'like angry grey ghosts'. The rest of the answer is open; look for clear reasons why it is or isn't an effective simile.

f 'grey ghosts' or 'hurl handfuls'.

g Look for responses that make it clear the learner has understood the meaning of the poem and the setting.

h A cat. Learners may feel that cats are often sleepy, like the poet, and also they like fish.

i Learners should pick up that 'tickles' is a stronger and more unusual verb than 'shines', and it also suggests a happy, playful atmosphere.

3 Learners' own answers. Ensure that learners give a reason for their choice.

Give learners access to some more poetry books, and ask them to find another poem that they like, about the sea or about another aspect of nature.

Extension: Learners could write or present a short piece comparing their chosen poem to one or more of the poems in this unit, saying which poem they prefer and why, and noting any differences or similarities.

Support: Learners could work in groups or pairs, and practise reading the poem they have found out loud. Their reading should demonstrate that they have understood the poem. If they struggle with this, help them with any parts of the poem that are difficult.

Unit 3 • The power of the sea

Workbook pages 17–18

Reading

Play the audio recording of the poem to the class. Help the class to hear the rhythm in the poem which echoes the movement and sounds of the sea. Ask how each verse in the poem begins. (with a question) Ask if any words are repeated. (rough) Let learners suggest why.

1–2 Let the learners read the poem aloud in pairs. Allow them to discuss the poem briefly. Learners could answer the questions in the Workbook for homework.

Student's Book page 28

Using similes

1–2 Use the prompts in the Student's Book to help learners understand how similes work. As a whole class, think up some similes using 'like' and 'as', and write them on the board. Then learners can tackle the open questions in the Student's Book independently or in groups.

Workbook page 18

Figurative language

1–2 Learners could complete the Workbook questions on similes and alliteration in class or for homework.

As an additional task, ask learners which of the figures of speech they preferred from page 18 of the Workbook. Ask learners to write a sentence about themselves and another one about a friend, reminding them to use 'like' or 'as' if they write similes.

Student's Book page 29

Reading and writing

1–2 Learners can read the information about haiku and tanka and complete the questions, either now or in preparation for the poetry writing activity below.

Use this exercise as an opportunity to practise splitting longer words up into syllables. Ask learners to clap the syllables in longer words from the haiku and tanka on page 29, for example: 'scatt/er/ing', 'wild/flow/ers', 'sudd/en/ly'. Ask learners to listen to the words and tell you which syllable in each one is stressed the most. (In all three of these words, the main stress falls on the first syllable – this is commonly the case in multisyllabic words in English.) Ask students to think of some more multisyllabic words, clap the syllables and identify the stressed syllables.

Student's Book page 30

Using verbs and adjectives

Remind learners about adjectives and adverbs by using the guidance in the Student's Book, page 33.

Learners can then complete the Student's Book activity individually or in their groups.

Unit 3 • The power of the sea

d Adverb: gently. Accept any reasonable choice of alternative adverb.

Student's Book page 30

Writing

1–4 Use the prompts in the Student's Book to introduce the task, and then ask learners to attempt the drafting and writing of their poem individually or in groups or pairs. Encourage learners to use the information about haiku and tanka on page 29 for support, if they choose to write poems in one of these forms. Offer help to any groups that are struggling, and allow time for refining and re-drafting the poems before learners prepare a final version.

You could also give learners a copy of PCM 8 to use as they prepare to write the poem. Learners can choose a photograph or a piece of music, and imagine they are inside the music or picture. They can then fill in the chart with descriptive words and phrases that show what they would see, hear, feel, taste and smell.

Remind learners about similes and alliteration. Make sure they understand that similes compare two things by using the words 'like' or 'as … as' (for example: 'the wind roared like a lion'; 'the sea was as smooth as a mirror'). Practise thinking of some alliterative phrases together, where a group of words start with the same initial letter, for example: 'cool, clear, crystal stream', 'wild, wet, windy weather'.

Encourage each group to add a picture to their poem, and display the finished poems on the classroom wall.

Weekly review

Use this rubric to assess learners' progress as they work through the activities this week. You can use the activities suggested beneath the table to follow up on your on-going assessment.

Level	Reading	Writing	Speaking and listening
■	Sometimes struggles to decode unfamiliar words and may have difficulty understanding some of what they read on a first reading.	Can write simple poems but needs help with choice of vocabulary and using features of poems such as rhyming.	Needs support to listen and requires prompting in order to respond appropriately.
●	Usually reads accurately and fluently, with some appropriate expression. May need support to read more unfamiliar or challenging texts.[1]	Writes poems with some confidence and attempts to find and use powerful words when prompted.	Demonstrates attentive listening. Listens carefully and responds appropriately.
▲	Reads with accuracy, fluency and appropriate expression, and may be able to comment in accurate detail on what they have read after a first reading.	Writes poems with confidence using features such as rhyming and often includes powerful words, sometimes unprompted.[1]	Demonstrates attentive listening and engages with another speaker. Listens carefully and responds appropriately.

Reading[1] Pair learners with a more confident learner and let pairs read additional poems out aloud to build confidence.

Writing[1] Encourage learners to write a simple rhyming poem, haiku or tanka about their local area or the view they can see from their window. Some learners should be able to do this activity independently and choose a different style of poem from the one they chose for the main writing activity. Other learners may choose to write the same type of poem that they wrote for the main writing activity. They can work in a group, and may choose to present their poem orally rather than in writing.

Unit 3 • The power of the sea

Week 2

Key strands and substrands: Lesson outcomes

Reading

- Read explanatory texts and understand their features and purposes
- Understand the difference between fiction and non-fiction texts
- Identify key features of non-fiction texts, including paragraphs
- Find key words and information in texts to answer questions
- Identify and explore adverbs and adverbial phrases
- Understand meanings in texts
- Explore words with common roots and record them in spelling logs
- Explore how verbs are used in texts

Writing

- Build words with related roots and meanings
- Use adverbs and adverbial phrases

Speaking and listening

- Sequence information for better understanding
- Use precise vocabulary
- Evaluate own and others' talk

Resources

- Student's Book pages 31–34
- Workbook pages 19–23
- PCM 9: Word families
- Slideshow: *Tsunami*
- Audio file: *Tsunami*

Introduction

Bring in some explanation texts, or use the example in the Workbook, page 19. Discuss with the group what an explanation text is for, and how it differs from instructions. For example, explanation texts normally explain a process; unlike instructions, they don't tell readers exactly how to carry out the process for themselves. They normally consist of statements in the present tense, rather than imperative/order sentences like instructions.

With the group, look at the examples of explanation texts. Draw learners' attention to any diagrams or helpful illustrations that show the process. Ask learners why they think explanation texts often include pictures. How do the pictures help?

Student's Book pages 31–32

Reading and writing

1 Introduce the explanation text on tsunamis in the Student's Book. Look at the way the text is organised. Ask learners why they think there are numbered sections. (To explain the process clearly and in a sequence.) Briefly elicit what learners already know about tsunamis, and then allow time for them to read the text independently or in pairs. Circulate as learners read the text silently, and answer any questions they have.

2 Learners can then answer the comprehension questions in their groups.

Answers

2   **a** non-fiction
    b Japan
    c an earthquake
    d low
    e slowly
    f Because the water gets shallower.
    g towering
    h Learners should notice that the tsunami can damage houses, buildings and land.
    i Accept any reasonable headings. Example headings: 1) Starting with an earthquake; 2) Long waves form; 3) A wall of water; 4) Damage and devastation.
    j Learners should realise that the diagrams help to explain the process – because the process is quite complicated, the pictures make it easier to understand than words alone.

Student's Book page 32

Listening and speaking

1–2 Give learners time to practise describing the process to their partners. Circulate and listen to some of the explanations. Invite some of learners to explain how tsunamis are formed to the whole class.

Unit 3 • The power of the sea

Workbook page 19

Reading and writing

1–2 Learners could complete this in class or for homework.

> #### Answers
> **2 a** Separate off the cream.
> **b** Shaken or stirred vigorously.
> **c** The liquid that forms when butter is made.
> **d** After the butter is solid.

Workbook page 20

Verb tenses

1–4 Learners could complete the Workbook activity on tenses and the verb *to be*, in class or for homework.

> #### Answers
> **1** present
> **2** Butter <u>is</u> made from milk. First, the cream <u>is</u> separated from the milk. The cream <u>is</u> put into a container and shaken, or churned, until it gets thick.
> **3** Butter was made from milk. First, the cream was separated from the milk. The cream was put into a container and shaken, or churned, until it got thick.
> **4 a** The boys were playing cricket on the beach.
> **b** Last Wednesday the weather was very hot.
> **c** We are going to the playground after school.
> **d** In the future, we will be able to live on the Moon.
> **e** I am bringing my little sister with me, because Mum and Dad are out shopping.

Student's Book page 33

Using adjectives and adverbs

1–4 If you haven't already used it, use the information on adverbs and adjectives on page 33 to remind learners of the difference between these types of words. Then ask learners to complete the activities independently or in pairs.

Extend the work on adverbs by introducing the idea of adverbial phrases. Explain that these are groups of words that work a bit like adverbs, by adding extra information to a verb. For example, you could add the adverb 'slowly' to the verb 'walk' (walk slowly), or you could add an adverbial phrase such as 'with

quick steps' (walk with quick steps). Encourage learners to think of some adverbial phrases of their own, which could be used to fill the gaps in questions 3 a, c and f.

> #### Answers
> **1** Adjectives: grey, happy, sparkling, dark, fabulous, shallow, big. Adverbs: sadly, gently, dangerously, hungrily, quickly.
> **2 a** huge, gigantic; **b** tired, exhausted; **c** hungry, ravenous
> **3** An open question; accept any reasonable adverb or adjective to fill each gap.
> **4 a** Tsunamis <u>sweep rapidly</u> across the ocean.
> **b** My boat <u>bobs gently</u> on the waves.
> **c** The rain <u>lashes roughly</u> against the windows.

Workbook page 21

Adjectives, adverbs and adverbial phrases

1–3 Learners could attempt these activities either in class or as homework.

> #### Answers
> **1 a** Jake <u>bravely dived</u> into the (deep) (green) pool.
> **b** Sasha's sister Kia was (small,) but (noisy.)
> **c** I <u>looked both ways carefully</u> before crossing the (busy) road.
> **d** The trees were <u>waving about furiously</u> in the (strong) wind.
> **2** Adjectives: beautiful, strange, scary, enormous. Adverbs: loudly, quickly, sleepily, fiercely.
> **3** Accept any sentences using the given adjectives and adverbs appropriately.

Student's Book page 34

Spelling

Use the prompts in the Student's Book to introduce the topic of word families. Write up another word family on the board and invite learners to come and add words (for example, the *please* word family includes *pleasure, pleasant, unpleasant, displease, pleasing*).

1–2 Then learners can complete the Student's Book activities either independently or as a whole group.

Unit 3 • The power of the sea

Workbook pages 22–23

Spelling

1–3 Learners could attempt these activities either in class or as homework.

Encourage learners to build up word families for as many different root words as possible. Give them copies of PCM 9 to support this. When all learners have created at least one word family, make a wall display and look as a whole group for spelling patterns and rules that show how the spelling of the root word varies with different suffixes and prefixes.

Extension: Learners will be able to include words which share a root and meaning but which have a different spelling from the root word (for example understanding that pleasure comes from the same root as please).

Support: Learners may stick to word families where the root word is varied only by adding suffixes and prefixes.

Weekly review

Use this rubric to assess learners' progress as they work through the activities this week. You can use the activities suggested beneath the table to follow up on your on-going assessment.

Level	Reading	Writing	Speaking and listening
■	May need support to follow the concepts in an unfamiliar explanation text. May need to be reminded to use the pictures as well as the words to gain information.[1]	Can identify and use adverbs, adverbial phrases and adjectives with support, not always completely accurately. Beginning to understand the concept of word families.	Needs support to make an explanation and describe a process in sequence.[1]
●	Can tackle most unfamiliar texts, reading silently and usually with concentration. May need support to put their understanding into words.	Can normally use adverbs, adverbial phrases and adjectives with some accuracy, and can self-correct when prompted. Can contribute ideas and words when putting together word families.	Can make a simple and fairly clear explanation and describe a process in sequence.
▲	Tackles both familiar and unfamiliar texts with confidence, reading silently and with concentration. Generally able to express their understanding clearly in words.	Can identify and use adverbs, adverbial phrases and adjectives accurately. Shows a clear understanding of the concept of word families.	Can make a simple explanation clearly and with an appropriate level of detail.[2]

Unit 3 • The power of the sea

> **Reading[1]** Work through page 19 in the Workbook with a small group of learners if they haven't yet completed this page. Let them answer the questions orally first, with some prompting if necessary.
>
> **Speaking and listening[1]** Ask learners to think of a process that they understand well, for example how a seed turns into a young plant, and explain it orally to a partner. Let them rehearse a short presentation on the process in pairs.
>
> **Speaking and listening[2]** Learners can do some research of their own about something to do with the sea and give a very short presentation to the class. For example: Why are there waves in the sea? Why are waves bigger on some days of the month?

Week 3

> ## Key strands and substrands: Lesson outcomes
>
> ### Reading
> - Explore and recognise how points are sequences and linked to develop ideas and paragraphs
>
> ### Writing
> - Plan and develop an explanation, using appropriate language and features
> - Write explanations in a logical sequence, with sections, links and organisational features
> - Use specialised vocabulary
>
> ### Speaking and listening
> - Give an accurate explanation, using precise vocabulary
> - Sequence information for better understanding
> - Adjust language and tone to audience
>
> ### Resources
> - Student's Book pages 35–38
> - Slideshow: *How sand is made*

Student's Book pages 35–36

Reading, speaking and writing

1–2 Ask learners to read the explanatory diagrams about how sand is made, either independently or in small groups or pairs. Listen and support learners as necessary, while they explain the process to their groups/partners.

Before learners turn their explanations into writing, use the board to model how to lay this out, with four clear sections, each with a heading. Encourage learners to work independently as far as possible; some learners may benefit from working in a pair or small group.

Student's Book pages 37–38

Writing

Step 1: Planning

Ask learners to follow the prompts in the Student's Book as they plan their explanation text. Depending on the support and research materials you have available in school, you may want to guide them towards particular topics on this list; however, if learners are enthusiastic and knowledgeable about particular subjects, encourage them to follow these up.

Learners could work in groups, in pairs or individually. It may help to divide learners up into pairs or groups depending on the topics they have chosen to focus on.

Allow time for research, and support learners as they gather information. You may need to remind them to focus on information that helps to explain the process, rather than general information about their chosen topic. Encourage them to use their explanations about sand as a model for this.

Remind learners that they need a clear structure, with a heading for each step in the process.

Give learners the opportunity to write a full draft of their piece, including diagrams. You could choose to review the pieces at draft stage so that you have the opportunity to give learners pointers for improving their work.

Extension: Learners may be able to write a longer and more complex explanation, possibly including some extra background information about the topic, as well as a range of helpful diagrams or illustrations.

Unit 3 • The power of the sea

Support: Work with learners to help them structure their work. These learners could write a briefer text, possibly with most of the information conveyed via labelled diagrams. They could use their diagrams as the basis of an oral presentation rather than a long piece of writing.

Step 2: Redrafting and revising

Encourage learners to use the checklist on page 12 of the Student's Book to help them revise their own writing, before sharing it with their partner or group. Remind learners of the rules for commenting on other people's work (see Teacher's Guide page 38).

Allow time for learners to redraft and revise their writing. Circulate among the groups and offer help as necessary. Remind learners to take care with the presentation of their pieces and to make sure their diagrams are clear and easy to follow.

Share all the explanation texts with the class, and display them on a noticeboard for everyone to read.

Thinking time

Let the learners reflect on the feedback they received on their work. Was it useful? Did it help them to improve their text? Ask individual learners to give examples of words or sentences they have changed as a result of feedback. Do the rest of the class agree it improves the text?

Weekly review

Use this rubric to assess learners' progress as they work through the activities this week. You can use the activities suggested beneath the table to follow up on your on-going assessment.

Level	Reading	Writing	Speaking and listening
■	May need support to read and understand unfamiliar text and may sometimes struggle to explain understanding.[1]	Can write a short and simple explanation text based on information read, with support if necessary.	At times needs support to contribute ideas and articulate thoughts in discussion, or when preparing a presentation.
●	Can read most texts with some confidence and accuracy. May sometimes need support to put understanding into words.	Can write a simple explanation text based on information read, mostly with accurate grammar and spelling.	Can normally contribute appropriately (though sometimes briefly) to a discussion or presentation, fleshing out ideas when prompted.
▲	Reads with accuracy and fluency, and can normally explain understanding of the text with little help or prompting.	Can write a more extended explanation text with accuracy and fluency, adding own ideas to information they have read.[1]	Contributes independently and appropriately to discussions and presentations.

Reading[1] Read the text *How sand is made* aloud with small groups of learners. Read one section at a time. Let learners describe the pictures, read the labels and then explain what each picture shows before moving on to the next section.

Writing[1] Learners could explore how to rewrite the text *How sand is made* in a different format. They could make a simple flow chart for example.

Unit 3 • The power of the sea

Task sheet 1

For consolidation and reinforcement, and to assess learners' understanding of the main learning objectives in Units 1, 2 and 3, have learners complete Task sheet 1. Mark and record the task as part of your on-going assessment. See page 6 Assessment in Primary English for guidance.

Marking guidance

Question 1

Reading

A handlebars (1)

B dancing (1)

C Any two from: 'just a touch of stiffness', 'as though neither of you were sure of the steps', 'you wobble', 'hanging on for dear life', 'all that kept you from falling'. (2)

D A description in the learner's own words that shows they have understood the scene shows someone riding a bike in the street. (2 – one mark for describing the scene accurately, and one for using their own words rather than quoting from the text)

E Accept any reasonable summary of how the poem makes the learner feel, provided reasons are given. (2 – one mark for saying how it makes them feel, and one for giving comprehensible reasons related to the text)

Question 2

Spelling, grammar and punctuation

A leading, hanging, dancing, falling (2 – allow half a mark for each correct word)

B
grip – gripping
extend – extending
wobble – wobbling
keep – keeping (2 – allow half a mark for each correct spelling)

C Any two from: 'as though', 'with', 'then', 'as if' (1 – allow half a mark for each correct connective)

D "You must grip them carefully,
both at the same time
as though you were leading
a partner onto the dance floor." (2 – allow one mark if both opening and closing speech marks are present and correctly placed, and one mark for a full stop at the end)

E frightened: nervous, terrified
excellent: good, world-beating (2)

Question 3

Writing

A (4 – allow half a mark for each correctly identified fact/opinion)

- This is the world's most amazing bicycle. (opinion)
- It's ideal for nervous cyclists and people who are just learning to ride. (opinion)
- It has a lightweight titanium frame and chunky puncture-proof tyres. (fact)
- It comes in a range of colours including black, silver, turquoise, orange and flame-red. (fact)
- It can be used on every type of surface – including roads, fields, mountains and even sandy beaches. (fact)
- It is every cyclist's dream. (opinion)
- It stops automatically if the rider is in danger. (fact)
- If you fall off or crash, the bike's built-in crash pads activate automatically and catch you. (fact)

B
Accept any persuasive advertisement that fulfils the brief in the question. Allow one mark for each of five sentences. Each sentence should contain either a fact, an opinion and/or an example of persuasive language. (5)

Unit 4 Other people, other places

Unit overview

This unit introduces learners to a range of stories from different cultures: Eritrean, Kenyan and Native American. Learners will listen to and read stories and answer comprehension questions. They will learn about the five-stage structure that many stories follow, and analyse stories using this structure. They will also explore and write alternative beginnings and endings for stories. They will review the use of apostrophes for possession, quantifiers, speech punctuation, adverbs and adjectives, and they will revise the correct formation of present, past and future tenses. They will learn how breaking longer words into syllables can help with spelling. They will finish the unit by planning and writing their own story based on the five-stage structure.

Introducing the unit

Talk with learners about how people all over the world have always loved to tell stories. Every country and area has its own traditional stories, and the old stories change over time as they are retold; meanwhile, new stories are always being created.

Explain that stories often tell us something about the place they came from. They may give us information about what the place is like, and what it is like to live there. Often, stories tell us something about the people who invented them, too – for example, the things they enjoy, and the difficulties and dilemmas they have faced.

Week 1

Key strands and substrands: Lesson outcomes

Reading

- Read and listen to traditional stories
- Recognise common words, including homophones
- Find information and meanings, and make inferences when reading
- Comment on figurative language
- Identify and understand quantifiers
- Identify the main parts of a story
- Explore apostrophes in texts
- Explain character and setting development
- Understand the layout of direct speech
- Comment on how fiction reflects the context in which it is set

Writing

- Use quantifiers
- Write alternative openings and endings for a story
- Begin to use correct punctuation in direct speech

- Spell homophones correctly
- Use apostrophes to show possession
- Write character profiles

Speaking and listening

- Listen and respond, making notes on a story
- Contribute to a discussion about setting and character
- Use speech and gestures to portray character

Resources

- Student's Book pages 39–43
- Workbook pages 24–27
- Slideshows: *The Clever Farmer*; *Abunuwasi's House*
- Audio files: *The Clever Farmer*; *Abunuwasi's House*
- PCM 10: *The Clever Farmer*
- PCM 11: The structure of a story
- Books or websites containing stories from around the world

Unit 4 • Other people, other places

Student's Book page 39

Listening and speaking

1–3 Tell learners that they are going to hear a story from Eritrea in Eastern Africa. The first time they hear the story, they can just listen and enjoy it; but on the second listening, they should make some notes about what the story tells us about the setting and characters. Ask learners to write these headings to help them structure their notes:

- Where the story is set
- What the place is like
- Who the main characters are
- What the characters are like.

Play the audio recording or read the story aloud to the class twice. The text of the story is on PCM 10. If you wish, you can give learners copies of the text so they can follow it as you read.

Allow time during and after the second reading, so that learners can discuss and make notes on the characters and setting in pairs. Encourage them to use exciting descriptive phrases to bring the characters and setting to life. Share the pairs' ideas with the whole class, and record the best words and phrases on the board for later. These words can be written in the learners' spelling logs.

Follow up by using some of the words and phrases describing the characters to make simple character profiles.

Workbook pages 24–25

Listening and speaking

1–4 Learners could complete this in class in their pairs, or independently for homework.

Learners create character profiles of the characters in the story *The Clever Farmer* that they have listened to. Explain the instructions to the class and then read the story again. Encourage them to take notes as they listen.

Answers
3 farmer, fields were full of dust and stones, watermelons shrivelled up, cow
4 Learners should describe the farm and the lack of water and food on the farm, which has caused crops to die, and the remaining cow.

Student's Book pages 40–41

Reading and writing

1 Learners work in pairs, reading the story silently at first and then taking turns to read it out loud to their partners. Circulate as they do this, so that you can help with any unfamiliar words.

Use the text to introduce or remind learners about homophones. The text contains the homophones *too/two/to*, *new/knew*, *their/there* and *know/no*. Ask learners to find these homophones in the text, and discuss the differences in meaning. Make a list of the homophones on the board and ask learners to help you write a sentence using each of them. Explain that when we are trying to work out which spelling of a homophone word to use, it helps to think about the meaning of the word and remember which spelling goes with which meaning.

2 Then ask learners to discuss the comprehension questions in their pairs, and write the answers. Many of the questions are open, but even for more closed questions always allow learners their own variations in the answers, as long as the sense of the answer is correct, and the language used is appropriate.

Answers
2 **a** In a town in Kenya
b Abunuwasi
c He wanted to leave town, and he needed the money so he could build or buy a new house somewhere else.
d He thought that if he didn't buy it, Abunuwasi might get fed up and leave town anyway, so that the merchant could get the whole house for free.
e In learners' own words: Abunuwasi wanted his friends to pretend that they were going to destroy the bottom half of the house, so that the merchant would think that his own half of the house was bound to be destroyed too, and so the merchant would buy the bottom part of the house in order to keep his own part safe.
f Accept any reasonable answer – learners should pick up that perhaps it was a good idea for Abunuwasi to move a long way away from the merchant, as well as anyone else he might have annoyed in the area.
g Learners should give a reason for their opinion.
h Accept any appropriate simile.

Unit 4 • Other people, other places

Extension and support: Talk about how traditional stories often use 'storytelling language' – they are written to sound like spoken stories. Share any examples of this that learners can think of, from stories they know. Let learners look for examples of storytelling language in another traditional story.

Thinking deeper

Take suggestions from learners about why stories are so valuable. Elicit that they give enjoyment to the reader or listener and they can also be educational.

Discuss why storytelling was so important in the past. Elicit from learners that not many people could read or write in the past and so telling stories was a form of entertainment and a way of bringing the community together. It was also a way of keeping the 'history' or traditions of a culture alive. Stories can have an educational value, often in the form of a moral or warning.

Take suggestions from the learners about how the author of *Abunuwasi's House* captures the idea of telling stories out loud. Ask them to give examples from the text.

Let learners work in groups to change the opening sentence of the story and then act it out to rest of the class.

Look for at least one example of spoken-style language in their opening sentence. Learners can peer review each of the groups.

Student's Book page 42

Punctuation, speaking and reading

1 Use the prompts in the Student's Book to remind learners how direct speech is punctuated. As a whole class, share some examples of correctly punctuated direct speech from books learners have been reading, and write them on the board. Then learners can tackle the first question in the Student's Book independently.

Allow time for learners to reread *Abunuwasi's House* and role-play the conversation. Share some of the role plays with the whole class, and draw learners' attention to some of the different ways of using words, tone of voice, facial expression and gesture to show how the merchant and Abunuwasi are

feeling. Which role plays do learners think are the most effective, and why?

2 Then ask the pairs to write out their conversations as correctly punctuated direct speech.

3 Learners act out the conversation between Abunuwasi and the merchant.

Answers

2 • "You've broken my best pen," said Abbie crossly.

• "No I haven't," said Li. "It was broken when I found it."

• "Never mind, Abbie. You can borrow my pen," said Nadine.

Workbook pages 25–26

Reading and writing

1 Learners can attempt this independently, either in class or as homework. Learners read the story *Abunuwasi's House* again and write a different ending for the story.

2 Learners turn the speech bubbles into direct speech, using speech marks.

Answers

2 "Come back," said the cat. "I only want to play with you."

"No thank you!" said the bird. "I know what your games are like!" (Accept correctly punctuated variants on this.)

Student's Book page 43

Reading and writing

Introduce the five-stage story structure using the prompts in the Student's Book. Make sure that learners understand the terminology before they move on to the comprehension exercise.

Give learners copies of PCMs 10 and 11, and ask them to work in groups to analyse *The Clever Farmer* using this structure – alternatively, you could do this as a whole class. Learners could use different coloured pens to show which parts of the story on PCM 10 belong in each stage of the story structure. Review this so that you can see whether learners have understood the concepts; if they haven't, you could work as a whole class and use PCM 11 to analyse another story that is already familiar to learners.

Unit 4 • Other people, other places

When they have understood the concepts, give each pair a clean copy of PCM 11 to help them analyse *Abunuwasi's House* using the five-stage structure, and ask them to sum up the relevant part of the story in each row of the chart.

Follow this up with an opportunity for learners to retell either *The Clever Farmer* or *Abunuwasi's House* in pairs or small groups. Give learners time to practise their retellings and work on making them really powerful and interesting. They can use their notes on PCM 11 to remind them of the story; encourage them to add their own details to interest the listener, and to choose their words carefully to help convey the emotions in the story.

Remind them to also use their voices, facial expressions and gestures to convey the story. Share some of the retellings with the whole class, and pick out some good aspects of each one to compare.

Student's Book page 43

Punctuation

Remind learners about apostrophes by using the guidance in the Student's Book on page 43. Learners can then complete the activity individually.

Answers
a Anna's eyes are blue and Ella's are brown.
b The girls' shoes are under their beds.
c Dad forgot to make the children's sandwiches.

d It's Michael's birthday, but he isn't very happy.
e I haven't seen Maria's sister today.

Workbook pages 26–27

Apostrophes and quantifiers

1 Learners can tackle activity 1 independently, either in class or as homework.

2 Learners choose the correct quantifier to complete each sentence.

Answers
1 a Jake's toys were all over the floor.
  b The children's faces were covered in chocolate.
  c The dragon's cave was dark and damp.
  d Mara's job was to fill up her pet hamsters' water bowl.
  e The girls' bicycles had flat tyres.
  f Eshe looked everywhere for Sam's lost bear.
  g The men's changing room was very crowded.
  h We scattered the chickens' food all over the yard.
  i The rabbit's leg was broken.
  j My mobile phone's battery is dead.
2 a either; b some; c all; d Both; e both; f some

Weekly review

Use this rubric to assess learners' progress as they work through the activities this week. You can use the activities suggested beneath the table to follow up on your on-going assessment.

Level	Reading	Writing	Speaking and listening
■	Sometimes struggles to decode unfamiliar words and may have difficulty recognising common words including homophones.[1]	Can write simple sentences, and attempt some punctuation of direct speech (not always accurately). Beginning to understand how to use apostrophes of possession.	Needs support to organise ideas and use language appropriately when storytelling.
●	Usually reads accurately and fluently and recognises most common words and some homophones. May need support to read more unfamiliar or challenging texts.	Can write in clear sentences, normally using basic sentence punctuation accurately. Knows how direct speech should be punctuated but does not always apply this accurately in writing. Can use apostrophes of possession accurately in simple contexts.	Uses some appropriate language, tone and gesture when storytelling, but sometimes needs reminding to keep the tone consistent.

© HarperCollins*Publishers* 2021

Unit 4 • Other people, other places

	Reads with accuracy, fluency, recognising common words and homophones.	Can write in clear sentences and has a good understanding of basic punctuation, including punctuation of simple direct speech. Almost always use apostrophes of possession accurately.	Demonstrates good simple storytelling ability, often with appropriate use of language, tone and gesture.[1]

Reading[1] Extract sentences with homophones from the story *Abunuwasi's House* or another familiar story. Write the sentences on the whiteboard and have learners identify the homophones. Then ask them to think of other words they know that sound the same. Let them suggest how to write the words and make sentences with the words.

Speaking and listening[1] Learners can use their storytelling skills to act out a different ending of the story *Abunuwasi's House or The Clever Farmer.*

Week 2

Key strands and substrands: Lesson outcomes

Reading
- Find information and meanings, and make inferences, when reading
- Identify the main parts of a story
- Understand and use spelling patterns (plurals and stress patterns)
- Understand verbs in present, future and past forms
- Explain character and setting development
- Predict what happens next in a story

Writing
- Plan and write part of a traditional story
- Make notes to use in writing
- Develop characters and viewpoint
- Write alternative beginning and endings to stories
- Use language for effect, including figurative language and adverbial phrases
- Use spelling strategies and generate spelling rules, including for words with prefixes and suffixes
- Keep a spelling log

- Find alternatives for overused words
- Explore shades of meaning in adjectives and adverbs
- Spell homophones
- Use verbs in the present, future and past forms correctly

Speaking and listening
- Read aloud with accuracy and expression, portraying characters through gesture and movement
- Contribute to a discussion about a story

Resources
- Student's Book pages 44–48
- Workbook pages 27–29
- Slideshow: *The Brave Baby*
- Audio file: *The Brave Baby*
- PCM 11: The structure of a story

Introduction

Explain that learners are going to read another story – this time a Native American one. The story has been told very simply, and they are going to use it as the basis for a retelling with some extra detail.

Student's Book pages 44–45

Reading and writing

1–2 When learners have read *The Brave Baby*, they can tackle the comprehension questions independently or in pairs.

Answers
2 a The chief was fierce and brave.
  b Open question, but he probably assumed that anyone who wasn't afraid of him would have to be a man.
  c She was calm; she played with her stick and smiled.
  d When the chief shouted at her.
  e He started to dance.
  f Less angry, and tired.

© HarperCollins*Publishers* 2021

Unit 4 • Other people, other places

Workbook pages 27–28

Writing

Discuss with learners how some words are 'overused'. Encourage them to always think of more exciting words when they writing to make their stories more interesting.

1–2 Encourage learners to complete activities 1 and 2 independently. The questions are open, so accept any appropriate and accurate use of adverbs and adjectives that fulfils the question criteria.

Encourage learners to use their notes dividing *The Brave Baby* into stages, to help them retell the story.

Extension: Learners should be able to retell the story fluently, and they may add extra dialogue or details, either remembered from the original story or invented.

Support: Learners may simply convey the main points of the story in order, with little elaboration. Prompt them, if necessary, to use appropriate storytelling language.

Answers
1 **a** small, asleep; **b** large; **c** cold; **d** hot; **e** old, angry
2 Learners' own answers

Student's Book page 46

Speaking, listening and writing

1–3 Introduce the activity using the prompts in the Student's Book. Allow plenty of time for learners to act out the story in their groups of three before they plan how to add extra detail to the story; acting it out will help them to understand the kinds of details it would be helpful to add.

Give learners copies of PCM 11 to help them make their notes on each section of the story. Review their notes and ideas before they go on to write their stories. This will enable you to see if they have understood what kinds of details to add. It may also

be helpful to get learners to act out the story in their groups again, with the extra bits, before they write.

4–5 Depending on how much time you have, you may want to ask learners to complete the writing activity quite quickly, as a preparation for the longer writing activity in Week 3. If time allows, however, they could spend longer on this, writing and reviewing a first draft before they work on a final draft which they can share with the rest of the class.

Student's Book page 47

Writing

1–2 Encourage all learners to tackle the questions. Accept any answers that use adjectives and adverbs appropriately and accurately. The activity can be done individually or through group discussion if learners need support.

Thinking deeper

Ask learners to imagine they are the chief for a day. Encourage them to think about how they would stand, talk and walk. Take ideas and let learners act out being the chief. This is fun activity, allow learners to spend time playing at being the chief. Bring learners back to their desks and ask them to write down ten words about how being the chief made them feel.

Student's Book pages 47–48

Spelling

1–2 Use the prompts in the Student's Book to introduce the idea of splitting longer words into syllables to help with spelling them. If necessary, remind learners about syllables by clapping the syllables in their names and in some other familiar words. Use the suggested spelling tips to analyse the spellings of some multi-syllable words from books learners have recently read, or work together on the list of words from *The Brave Baby* in the Student's Book.

Encourage learners to apply these strategies when they encounter new multi-syllable words. You could make a shared list of longer words split into syllables, and put it on the wall for reference.

Remind learners to write interesting or tricky words in their spelling logs.

Workbook pages 28–29

Spelling

1–4 Learners can complete the activities independently, in class or as homework.

Unit 4 • Other people, other places

Answers

1 **a** happily (3); **b** correct (2); **c** kicking (2); **d** somebody (3); **e** underneath (3); **f** beautiful (3)

2 **a** somebody; **b** whenever; **c** favourite; **d** everyone; **e** beautiful

3 **a** These are my new friends. They're from South America.

   b I've got too much homework to do.

   c Adwin is good at reading and writing.

   d I would love to go swimming.

   e I have been to Kuala Lumpur. Have you ever been there?

   f Dad is not here this evening.

4 Accept any sentences using the homophone words correctly.

Student's Book page 48

Using verb tenses

1–2 When learners have read *The Brave Baby*, they can tackle the activity independently or in pairs, refreshing their knowledge of the past, present and future tenses as well as direct speech.

Workbook pages 29–30

Verb tenses

1–3 Learners can complete the activities independently, in class or as homework.

Answers

1 **a** I was excited because it was my turn to go down the water slide.

   b Priti wore her best blue sari.

   c We walked into town.

   d Michael and Ruben argued again.

2 **a** Dad will be in New York.

   b I was nine on Saturday.

   c Sabah and Emily were the winners.

   d We will be happy to see Grandma.

3 **a** Mum became very cross when we got mud on the carpet.

   b I wrote my name carefully.

   c The dragon flew over the rooftops.

   d Ruth and Jacob came swimming with us.

   e A large parcel stood in the corner of the room.

Weekly review

Use this rubric to assess learners' progress as they work through the activities this week. You can use the activities suggested beneath the table to follow up on your on-going assessment.

Level	Reading	Writing	Speaking and listening
■	May need support to explain their understanding of a story when discussing it with others. Can retell a story in simple terms, sometimes with prompting.	Often needs support to write a new version of a known story; written retellings are simple and may miss some details.[1]	Needs support to tell stories effectively. When prompted, can use some simple storytelling language effectively.
●	Can contribute to a discussion about a story, and can attempt a retelling with little support. May sometimes need support to put their understanding into words.	Can tackle a simple retelling of a known story and may be able to add some extra details of own, with some support if necessary.	Can orally retell a simple story effectively, with some good use of voice and gesture and some appropriate storytelling language.
▲	Can contribute fluently to a discussion about a story, and can retell a story with minimal prompting and support.	Can retell a familiar story confidently, usually getting the sequence correct and adding appropriate details in places.[2]	Can orally retell a known story effectively, using their voices and choice of vocabulary effectively to engage the listener.

Writing[1] Allow learners to work up a group retelling of their new version of the story, and present it orally to the class instead of in writing.

Writing[2] Challenge learners to add extra dialogue to help draw the reader into the story. They should be able to sum up the message of the story briefly at the end.

Unit 4 • Other people, other places

Week 3

Key strands and substrands: Lesson outcomes

Reading

- Identify the main stages of a story
- Explore and recognise the key features of text structure and how ideas are organised in paragraphs
- Express personal responses to texts

Writing

- Plan a story
- Write character profiles
- Write different beginnings and endings for a story
- Punctuate direct speech

Speaking and listening

- Read aloud clearly
- Evaluate the work of others

Resources

- Student's Book pages 49–50
- Slideshow: *The Selkie Wife*
- Audio: *The Selkie Wife*
- PCM 11: The structure of a story
- PCM 12: *The Selkie Wife*

Introduction

For the main writing activity, learners will write their own version of a story that follows the five stages outlined earlier in this unit. There are several ways of tackling this, depending on the amount of support your class needs.

One option is to give learners access to a range of traditional tales from your own country or area, or from elsewhere around the world. You could let learners read a selection of stories and choose one to use as the basis of their own retelling – or you could select one or two appropriate stories yourself and ask the group to choose one of these.

Alternatively, learners could write their own new versions of *The Clever Farmer* or *Abunuwasi's House* (if they haven't already retold these in detail earlier in the unit). This option might be appropriate for learners needing more support.

A further option is to allow learners to make up their own new story which follows the five-stage story structure.

Student's Book pages 49–50

Writing

Prepare some cards with the five stages of a story structure written on them: Introduction, Problem/Build-up, Climax/Conflict, Resolution, Conclusion. Ask learners to put them in order. Display these in order and ask learners to suggest what each stage includes. Learners can then follow the prompts in the Student's Book as they plan their explanation text. They could work in groups, in pairs or individually. It may help to divide learners up into pairs or groups depending on

the story they have chosen to focus on, so that those working on the same story can support each other. Encourage plenty of discussion, and prompt learners to practise telling their story out loud – or even acting it out – before they begin their first written draft.

Encourage learners to think carefully about the main characters in their stories. Show them how to create a simple character profile with different headings such as 'appearance', 'how they act', 'how they speak', 'what other people think of them', and so on. They can make notes about their main characters under these headings, and then use some of this detail when they come to write their stories.

Support learners as they work on structuring their stories. They could use PCM 11 as a format for collecting their notes on what happens at each stage of the story. If necessary, model this note-taking process for them.

Because, ideally, learners should be trying to write a story that includes expressive language, interesting details and dialogue, it will take them more than one session to write a complete draft; so allow plenty of time for the planning and drafting stages.

Once learners have completed their drafts talk about the editing process. Learners should check the punctuation and spelling in their own writing first. Remind them that they should also always read through everything they have written to make sure it makes sense. Then learners can give their work to a partner for checking. The partner reads with a 'fresh pair of eyes' and alerts the writer to things that may not make sense and mistakes the writer may not have noticed. Remind learners of the need to be constructive and to find things to comment on positively as well as making suggestions for improvement. The learners can then make further improvements based on this feedback.

It is worth reading learners' stories yourself at draft stage too, if possible, so that you can also make suggestions.

After the redrafting stage, give learners the opportunity to write a full draft of their piece, including pictures if they wish. You could make a class book containing all the finished stories.

Extension: Learners should be able to write a longer and more complex story, adding believable dialogue and some interesting details they have thought of for themselves.

Support: Learners may write a shorter story, and it is likely to be quite close to the original model story in terms of language, dialogue and structure. They may need extra support at all stages of the project. Some groups may not be able to create a full written version of their story, in which case they could be invited to present the story orally to the class instead.

Thinking time

Let the class reflect on the stories they have read. They can say which story they liked the best and what they have learned about other cultures from the stories.

Weekly review

Use this rubric to assess learners' progress as they work through the activities this week. You can use the activities suggested beneath the table to follow up on your on-going assessment.

Level	Reading	Writing
■	May need support to read and understand an unfamiliar story, and may need support to analyse its structure and retell it.	Can summarise and retell a simple story with support.[1]
●	Can read most texts with some confidence and accuracy. May sometimes need support to put their understanding of structure into words.	Can write a retelling of a story, including some dialogue and other telling details, with occasional support[2]
▲	Reads with accuracy and understanding. Understands how the story fits the five-stage structure, and can explain understanding.	Can write a more extended retelling with accuracy and fluency, adding own ideas to improve the story.[3]

Give learners PCM 12, which is a very short outline of a Scottish story called *The Selkie Wife*. There is also a slideshow and audio of the story. Explain that a selkie is a mythical creature that is half-human, half-seal. Selkies are seals when they are in the sea, but they turn into humans when they take off their sealskin coats and step onto dry land.

Ask learners to use PCM 11 to help them analyse the story, so they can identify which parts of the story correspond to the five stages. They could present this either in chart form using PCM 11, or by highlighting or underlining the different sections in different colours.

The Selkie Wife fits the five-part structure like this:

- Introduction – paragraphs 1 and 2
- Problem/build-up – paragraphs 3 and 4
- Climax – paragraph 5
- Resolution – paragraph 6
- Conclusion – paragraph 7

Writing[1] Work with groups of learners and help them to identify the structure of the story.

Writing[2] Ask learners to retell the story after they have completed their analysis, adding details and dialogue to make it more interesting.

Writing[3] Learners could either write their own new version of the story, or retell it orally for an audience.

Unit 5 The only problem is ...

Unit overview

In this unit, learners will read stories and poems that deal with issues and dilemmas. They will read, perform and compare poems from different cultures, and will write their own poem in a similar style using these as models. They will read and answer comprehension questions on two stories that focus on children in difficult situations, and attempt a similar piece of writing of their own, dividing their story into clear paragraphs. They will practise spelling words with common letter strings but different pronunciations, and revise the grammar of statements, orders and questions. They will also explore powerful verbs and adjectives, and look at what a well-chosen adverb or adverbial phrase can add to a sentence.

Introducing the unit

Explain to learners that stories, plays and poems can often help us to think about difficult issues. If we are going through a difficult time, or have a problem, it can be very helpful to read about someone who has had a similar experience. Sometimes stories and poems about problems and dilemmas can also help us to think about how we would react if we ever found ourselves in difficult circumstances.

Encourage learners to contribute to a list of stories, films, and so on, that they have read or seen, which dealt with a problem or issue. You may be surprised how many stories fit this category! Sometimes, even fantasy stories (like Cressida Cowell's *How to Train Your Dragon* series) touch on real-life problems and dilemmas in a way that can be very interesting and helpful.

Week 1

Key strands and substrands: Lesson outcomes

Reading

- Read poetry and stories about issues and respond in a personal way
- Understand meaning in texts
- Understand characters and settings, and make inferences
- Identify point of view
- Locate and use relevant information to answer questions
- Comment on a writer's choice of words
- Suggest synonyms and identify powerful verbs
- Identify adverbs
- Understand subject-verb agreement in texts
- Explore examples of adverbs and adverbial phrases

Writing

- Explore and use adverbs and adverbial phrases
- Use verbs correctly
- Choose and use words to strengthen the impact of writing

Speaking and listening

- Read aloud with expression and accuracy
- Begin to take assigned roles in groups
- Plan and deliver a group presentation
- Change speech and use gestures to portray characters

Resources

- Student's Book pages 51–56
- Workbook pages 31–32
- Slideshows: *The Youngest*; *Meeting Mr Faulkner*
- Audio files: *The Youngest*; *Meeting Mr Faulkner*
- PCM 13: Reading aloud

Unit 5 • The only problem is ...

Student's Book pages 51–52

Reading, listening and speaking

1 Tell learners that they are going to listen to a poem by Michael Rosen. Read it aloud to the class with lots of expression, or play them the audio recording.

Ask learners what the narrator's main problem is in this poem, and clarify that it's about what it's like to be the youngest in the family, with a bossy big brother.

Then give learners time to read the poem aloud in their pairs, and discuss it using the prompts in the Student's Book. Walk around the class while they do this, so that you can check their understanding and make sure they are listening and responding appropriately to each other. Clarify any aspects of the poem that may be puzzling them.

2–3 The answers to the prompt questions are open, and largely a matter of personal opinion and interpretation, so accept any sensible responses. Encourage learners to back up their opinions with reasons, and quotations from the poem.

You may want to pause before they get to point 8 (choosing one of their stories to tell to the class). Encourage learners to make some notes to help them organise their story before they tell it. If they jot down the main points of the story in sequence, in about three to four sentences, this will help them to stick to the point and tell their story effectively.

When the pairs have had time to tell their stories, ask learners to practise reading the poem in groups of four. Give them time to read the poem through several times before they perform it, and listen to their practice readings so that you can give guidance if necessary.

Extension: Learners should be able to produce a lively group performance of the poem, with all members of the group contributing appropriately.

Support: Learners may need support in dividing the reading up between them, and help with working out how to read some of the lines expressively. PCM 13 contains a checklist to help learners with expressive reading; this may be a useful prompt for some groups.

Student's Book pages 53–54

Reading

1 Before learners work independently to read *Meeting Mr Faulkner* and answer the questions on it, ask them to read the title of the story and look at the picture. Ask: *Who are the characters? How old are they? How are they related? What does the man have in his hand? Why is one girl standing in the doorway?* Then ask them to predict what they think the story is about.

2 You could read the text aloud to the whole group (or play the audio recording). This may help learners to understand the text, if some of the idiom used is unfamiliar to them. Circulate as they go on to read independently, so that you can check that they understand and help with any unfamiliar words. Then ask learners write the answers to the questions.

3 Many of the questions are open, but even for more closed questions, always allow learners their own variations in the answers, as long as the sense of the answer is correct, and the language used is appropriate.

Answers

3 a Kitty's viewpoint

b 'I saw Jude's eyes widen to saucers' or 'Jude rushed upstairs, clutching her booty to her chest'.

c Open question; learners may feel that Kitty isn't quite sure whether she likes Gerald yet, and maybe she is worried or unhappy at the idea of her mum having a new friend like him.

d He doesn't show any sign of being worried about it – he cleverly speaks in such a way that Kitty doesn't have to answer if she doesn't want to.

e Open question; accept any reasonable response.

f 'Just then Floss padded in through the front door, and started rubbing up against his trouser legs as if she'd known and loved him all her life' or 'I was still trying to work it out (and Floss was still purring shamelessly) when Jude came thundering downstairs.'

g He doesn't know Floss's real name, but he doesn't want to ask Kitty what it is, so he uses 'Buster' as a nickname.

h Accept any reasonable synonyms for 'enraptured' and 'ambled'.

i Accept any three sentences from the text that use powerful verbs.

j An open question; accept any description that reflects the picture of Kitty built up in the text.

Unit 5 • The only problem is ...

Workbook page 31

Reading

1–2 Learners could complete this activity as a follow-up to reading *Meeting Mr Faulkner*. Some learners will be able to complete this activity independently for homework; other learners may benefit from completing it in groups, with some assistance as necessary.

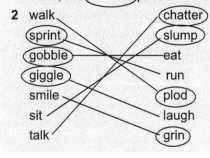
Student's Book pages 55

Using adverbs

Use the prompts in the Student's Book to remind learners how adverbs and adverbial phrases are used. Encourage learners to think of an adverb each, and write their adverbs on the board. Then, as a whole group, think of a sentence using each adverb.

Take one of your sentences and change the adverb into an adverbial phrase (a group of several words that adds extra information about the verb). For example:

- adverb: angrily
- sentence: I threw my bag down angrily.

- new sentence with adverbial phrase: I threw my bag down with an angry thump.

1–3 Learners can complete the questions in the section on adverbs independently.

Extension: Ask learners to rewrite these sentences, adding an adverb or adverbial phrase to each one:

- I ate my breakfast.
- He stepped inside.
- Carlo stopped.

Workbook page 32

Adverbs

1–3 Learners could attempt these activities independently, either in class or as homework. Review their work to make sure that they have understood how to use adverbs correctly.

Unit 5 • The only problem is …

Student's Book page 56

Subject-verb agreement

Use the prompts in the Student's Book to remind learners about subjects, objects and agreement of subject and verb. Ask learners to say some simple sentences, like 'I enjoy Maths' or 'I saw a fox'. Write their sentences on the board and invite them to underline the subject, draw a wiggly line under the verb and draw a circle round the object. Then write some sentences where the subject and verb do not agree (e.g. 'Ducks is swimming on the river', 'My cat are hungry') and invite learners to correct these by adding the right form of the verb to go with the subject.

1–2 Then learners can attempt the Student's Book activities independently.

Answers
1 **a** My hamster is eating.
   b The children are playing.
   c I am tired.
2 **a** I ate the cake. (subject 'I', verb 'ate', object 'the cake')
   b The boys were wearing sports clothing. (subject 'the boys', verb 'were wearing', object 'sports clothing')
   c Miss Beckson was angry with Class 2. (subject 'Miss Beckson', verb 'was angry', object 'Class 2')

Weekly review

Use this rubric to assess learners' progress as they work through the activities this week. You can use the activities suggested beneath the table to follow up on your formative assessments.

Level	Reading	Writing	Speaking and listening
■	May need support to pay attention to sentence grammar and punctuation in order to read aloud fluently.	May need further practice to understand how verbs need to agree with subjects. May need support to remember all the relevant aspects of grammar, spelling and punctuation when writing their sentences.	May find it difficult to read a poem out loud with appropriate expression and fluency.[1] Needs support to organise ideas and use language appropriately when conveying ideas in a whole-class or large group setting.
●	May need support to read and fully understand more unfamiliar or challenging texts.	Understands verb-subject agreement but makes some mistakes. Writes own simple sentences conforming to most of the relevant grammar, spelling and punctuation rules.	Usually reads aloud accurately and fluently, with some appropriate expression. Can tell a simple story in a whole-class or large group setting, mostly sticking to the point and using appropriate language.
▲	Shows good understanding of what they have read.	Understands and uses verb-subject agreement correctly. Shows a good understanding of basic punctuation, grammar and spelling.	Reads aloud with accuracy, fluency and appropriate expression, creating an interesting experience for the listener.[2] Demonstrates good simple storytelling ability, using voice, facial expressions and vocabulary choices effectively.

Speaking and listening[1] Play the audio of the poem again a few times or read the poem and let learners read along with you to build up confidence.

Speaking and listening[2] Let learners work in pairs and find another poem about a problem. They can practise the poem and read it aloud for the enjoyment of the rest of the class.

Unit 5 • The only problem is …

Week 2

Key strands and substrands: Lesson outcomes

Reading

- Find explicit and implicit meaning, and make inferences about a poem
- Compare poems and express preferences
- Notice how time or context is reflected in texts
- Recognise features of poems
- Understand links in texts

Writing

- Plan and write a poem
- Use appropriate layout, content and language in writing

- Express a point of view
- Evaluate own and others' writing

Speaking and listening

- Read aloud with expression, showing awareness of punctuation

Resources

- Student's Book pages 57–59
- PCM 13: Reading aloud
- PCM 14: Write your own poem
- Slideshow: *Eleven Years Old*
- Audio file: *Eleven Years Old*

Introduction

Explain to learners that they are going to read a poem by Dionne Brand. You may choose to read or play this poem to the whole class before learners reread the poem independently or in pairs. Allow time for learners to read the poem twice before they answer the comprehension questions.

Student's Book pages 57–58

Reading and writing

1–2 When learners have read the poem, they can tackle the comprehension questions independently or in pairs.

Extension: Learners should be able to answer the comprehension questions independently with minimal support.

Support: Learners may benefit from discussing the questions with a partner before they write.

Answers

2 a Yams and goats.

b Because her grandmother feels she is old enough at eleven years old, and her family needs her to help keep the farm going.

c Learners should understand that she feels a bit reluctant or ambivalent, because the work is hard and perhaps she feels she is still quite young at eleven. She would probably rather be going to school – we know this because she is looking forward to a future where this is possible.

d It means that it will not stop your mind from working.

e Accept any answer that makes connections between the learner's life and the life of the child in the poem, and draws out at least one similarity and one difference.

f Possible similarities include: both poems are from a child's point of view; both poems are written in very natural, speech-like language; both poems are about a problem the narrator has; both poems are about family relationships.

g Possible differences include: the narrator of the first poem is a boy and the second poem is a girl; the problem is more serious in the second poem; the first poem is about an experience that is common everywhere whereas the problem in the second poem only affects children in some parts of the world.

Student's Book page 58

Listening and speaking

1–4 Introduce the activity using the prompts in the Student's Book. Allow plenty of time for learners to practise reading and performing their chosen poem in their pairs before they perform it. Encourage learners to make some notes about their reasons for choosing their poem, and to practise explaining their reasons as well as practising the poem performance. You could give copies of PCM 13 to the pairs as a prompt to help them prepare for performance.

Encourage learners to review their own and others' performances. They should think of at least one thing they liked, and one thing they would change if they performed their piece again.

Student's Book page 59

Writing

Remind the learners about some of the features of poems. Focus on the choice of interesting adjectives, adverbs and verbs and on words or groups of words that are repeated. Learners may also know that some poems have rhyming lines and a certain rhythm.

Ask learners to think about how they will present the poem. Will they write it by hand or will they type it on a computer? Will they use different fonts and colours in the layout?

The writing activity on PCM 14 offers a more scaffolded approach to writing a poem. There are various ways of organising this work, depending on the needs of learners.

Support:

- You could ask learners to complete the PCM before they tackle the Student's Book writing activity.
- You could use the PCM as the basis for a whole-class or large group poem, which would give you the opportunity to model the process for any learners or groups who might otherwise struggle with this.
- You could ask learners to complete the PCM instead of the Student's Book activity.
- You could ask learners to complete the PCM after doing the Student's Book activity, as reinforcement.

The answers to the PCM are open. The final poem should be written on paper.

The Student's Book prompts take learners through the more open-ended writing activity in some detail. Allow plenty of time for them to complete all the stages, including the revision stage.

Extension: Learners may be able to use the Student's Book prompts to structure their writing with little extra support.

Support: It may be necessary to work with learners to make sure they understand all the steps and know what they need to do.

Celebrate learners' completed poems by creating a class display of their illustrated final work, and/or organising a performance session where everyone who wishes to can read their finished poem to the class.

Weekly review

Use this rubric to assess learners' progress as they work through the activities this week. You can use the activities suggested beneath the table to follow up on your on-going assessment.

Level	Reading	Writing	Speaking and listening
■	Needs support to answer questions and make comparisons	Needs support to use model to write poem and choose poetic features.[1]	Needs practice and support to prepare a performance.[1]
●	Able to work with partner to answer most questions and make basic comparisons between poems.	Can work mostly independently to write a poem based on a clear model, though may need some support to include poetic features such as repeating lines and interesting choices, and so on.	Can work on a good straightforward performance of a poem with minimal support.
▲	Works independently to answer questions about poem and make comparisons.	Can write an effective short poem based on a clear model, and will often include poetic features such as repeating lines, well-chosen vocabulary, and so on.	Can work mostly independently to produce an effective performance of a simple poem.

Writing[1] Use a few lines from a poem as a writing frame. Let learners replace some of the words in the lines with words of their own. Then prompt them to add their own lines or words to the poem.

Speaking and listening[1] Make copies of the poem and help learners to makes notes on the poem which will prompt them as they read. They could underline the words that need emphasis or use little drawings to show where they need to make gestures.

Unit 5 • The only problem is ...

Week 3

Key strands and substrands: Lesson outcomes

Reading

- Read different types of fiction
- Find explicit and implicit meaning, and make inferences
- Understand how texts are organised and ideas are linked in paragraphs
- Record interesting words

Writing

- Explore short vowel phonemes
- Use different strategies to spell words, including words with different letter strings
- Plan and write about an issue
- Develop a logical sequence of ideas, using paragraphs

- Write alternative beginnings to stories
- Explore and use alternatives for overused words
- Begin to express viewpoint
- Evaluate own and others' writing

Speaking and listening

- Use non-verbal communication techniques

Resources

- Student's Book pages 60–62
- Workbook pages 33–36
- Slideshow: *The New Boy*
- Audio files: *The New Boy*

Student's Book page 60

Reading

Before learners read *The New Boy* independently or in pairs, briefly discuss how they think it might feel to have just arrived in a new country, as well as a new school, not being able to speak the same language as everyone else. If any of the learners have experienced this situation themselves, invite them to talk about it if they wish to (but don't pressurise them to share their experiences if they would rather not).

Student's Book page 61

Comprehension

Read *The New Boy* to the class, or play the audio, before learners tackle the text and questions for themselves. You may want to explain that the author of this story, Jamila Gavin, moved from India to the UK as a child, so her own experiences colour her writing. If learners are interested, you can do some research to find out more about this award-winning author.

Answers

a Hindi

b Open question; learners may say that he is used to sitting on the ground, not at a table, or that he might be feeling awkward because he is new to the school.

c Because he is used to living somewhere with far fewer big buildings, cars, etc., where you can see the sky and the ground and where food is grown locally.

d Open question; accept any three differences that are supported by the text.

e Open question; learners may feel that it is because the other children are pleased that Amrik is trying to speak English, and they find what he has said/the way that he said it amusing. If learners feel that it is because they are teasing Amrik, point out that the text doesn't really show much evidence of that – though of course some people might well want to tease a new boy in this situation.

f Open question; accept any two reasonable ideas for ways of helping Amrik settle in.

g Open question; learners may say that the author's personal experience of moving to Britain from India give her writing more emotion, and make it more true-to-life.

Workbook page 33

Writing

1 Learners can work in groups and discuss an alternative beginning to the story *The New Boy*. Then they can work alone and write their own alternative beginnings. Encourage them to share these with the class.

Unit 5 • The only problem is ...

2 As a challenge, learners could complete activity 2 in the Workbook. You could prepare a group of learners for this by discussing some of the things that Kamla and Kate could show Amrik and how this could be different to his experiences.

Student's Book page 61

Reading and writing

1–2 Remind learners about how paragraphs are used in fiction, using the prompts in the Student's Book if you wish. Look at some books in the classroom to find examples of new paragraphs being used for a new speaker, and new paragraphs being used when something new happens in the story.

You can use this as an opportunity to draw learners' attention to the similarities between paragraphs and chapters – both are used to organise ideas in a book, as generally authors start a new chapter when something exciting or important happens in a story.

Remind learners if necessary that when using paragraph breaks for direct speech, we only need a new paragraph when a new speaker starts – we don't need a paragraph break if the same speaker continues, even if there's a sentence or two with no speech, between their speeches. So in the last paragraph of the Workbook text, there is no new paragraph before '"We won't get far without these!"', because the speaker is still Charlie.

Review learners' work on paragraphs to make sure they have understood the rules for paragraph breaks when writing their own continuation to the story.

Answers
1   Paragraph 1: new event; paragraph 2: new event; paragraph 3: new speaker; paragraph 4: new speaker; paragraph 5: new event; paragraph 6: new speaker; paragraph 7: new speaker; paragraph 8: new speaker
2   An open question. Review learners' work so that you can check they have understood the rules for creating new paragraphs.

Workbook page 34

Reading and writing

Invite learners to complete this activity either in class or as homework.

Answers
Paragraph breaks are shown with a double oblique line below.

"Come on, Charlie," said Maya. "We're going to miss the bus!" // "Hang on!" snapped Charlie. "Give me a moment – I'm nearly ready." // "Well," said Maya, "I'm going to the bus stop. I'll see you there – if the bus doesn't get there before you do!" // Maya skipped off down the road to the bus stop. Her friend Patsy was already waiting there. // "Hi, Patsy!" yelled Maya. "Are you going to the match too?" // "Of course!" said Patsy. "I wouldn't miss it – it's not every day that your team gets to the final!" // Just then, Charlie came running up, panting and puffing. "I think you forgot something, Maya," he gasped. He was waving a pair of tickets for the match. "We won't get far without these!"

Student's Book page 61

Spelling

1–3 Tackle this activity together as a whole-class activity.

Ask learners to come up to the board and write down any *ou* words they find in the extract, so that you have a complete list. Then model how to group the words according to how the *ou* is pronounced.

Finish by spending five minutes looking through other written materials in the classroom for extra *ou* words. You could make the sorted lists of *ou* words into a permanent classroom display, so that learners can add more words to the appropriate list as they come across them in their reading. Learners can also add some of these to their spelling logs.

Answers
1 and 2
ou as in 'round':
ground; our; out; playground; around; plough
ou as in 'soup':
you;
ou as in 'would':
could;
ou as in 'country':
countryside

Unit 5 • The only problem is ...

ou as in 'flavour':
colour
3 Learners' own answers.

Invite learners to tackle the activity on words with the letter string *ough*, in groups or independently.

Answers to 'Words with ough' box
1 plough
2 cough
bought, ought, thought
rough, enough
borough, thorough
bough, drought
through
dough
enough
3 Encourage learners to add as many more *ough* words as possible to their lists.

Workbook page 35
Spelling

Learners can complete the Workbook spelling activity either in class or as homework.

Answers
1 *ea* as in 'head': dead, bread, breakfast, healthy, meadow, stealth, feather, thread, tread, spread, leather
ea as in 'teach': beach, seat, deal, heal, steal, leaves, feast, steam, reach, team, bead, treat, peak
ea as in 'steak': great, break
2 Open questions; accept any accurately spelled sentences that use the target words appropriately.

Workbook page 36
Writing

Discuss with learners how some words are 'overused'. Encourage them to always think of more exciting words when they writing to make their stories more interesting.

Learners could do this activity either in class or as homework, in preparation for the writing activity.

Answers are open, but use this as an opportunity to check that learners understand what constitutes a 'more interesting' word, and encourage them to use more adventurous word choices rather than overused words.

Student's Book page 62
Writing

Ask learners to undertake this activity as an end of unit review activity. Before they start, remind them how to use a paragraph plan: by thinking about the main point they wish to get across in each paragraph and writing this as a heading on the plan, and then making notes about what they will say in each paragraph under each heading.

You may prefer learners who are struggling with writing to work collaboratively in groups on the planning and revision aspects of this activity; encourage them to write their final piece independently, however, so you can use it to assess their skills and understanding.

Tell learners that they can write as themselves, saying how they think they would feel if they were in a similar situation to Amrik; or they can write in character as someone else.

Remind all learners that you are expecting them to choose their words carefully for this piece, and use interesting and exciting words wherever possible, so the reader can imagine what is happening very clearly.

Page 62 of the Student's Book gives a checklist of things to look out for when revising learners' pieces. Remind them also of the need to use their best joined handwriting in their final work, so that it is easy to read and looks good on display.

Support: Learners may need support to write their paragraph plans. You could talk them through the process as a group, modelling how you would go about planning this piece of work in paragraphs yourself, before they attempt to write their own plan.

Thinking time

Let learners reflect on what they have read in this unit. Ask what they have learned about how people feel when they have to deal with issues and dilemmas.

Unit 5 • The only problem is ...

Weekly review

Use this rubric to assess learners' progress as they work through the activities this week. You can use the activities suggested beneath the table to follow up on your on-going assessment.

Level	Reading	Writing
■	May need support to understand how stories are divided into paragraphs.[1]	Needs support especially at the planning stage, but can then write a simple recount using a paragraph plan.
●	Should be able to grasp the concept of paragraphing with limited support.[2]	Can write and plan a short imaginative recount with little support.
▲	Understands clearly the concept of paragraphing and can explain with minimal support how a text is divided into paragraphs.	Quickly grasps the concept of a paragraph plan and can independently apply this to their own short recount.

Reading[1] Make a copy of a familiar story that is divided into paragraphs. Cut the text up into paragraphs and let learners work in pairs to rearrange the text into paragraphs. Then talk about why the text is divided into paragraphs.

Reading[2] Choose a short story and remove the paragraphing (as in the Workbook on page 34). Let learners work in pairs, read the text aloud and discuss where paragraphs are needed and why.

Unit 6 Making the headlines

Unit overview

This unit explores a range of journalistic writing, giving learners the opportunity to read and write different types of newspaper and magazine articles, including news reports, non-chronological reports and instructions. Learners will discuss the texts in groups and answer comprehension questions before writing their own texts based on the models provided. They will learn about the key features of journalistic writing. They will practise techniques for spelling words with more than one syllable, find out how to use commas around phrases in parenthesis, and continue to explore the use of connectives.

Introducing the unit

Bring in examples of several different types of news reports to share with the learners. Display appropriate online reports as well as printed reports from magazines or newspapers. (Check through in advance to make sure there are no articles that would be inappropriate to share with learners; if necessary you can just choose the most appropriate parts of the paper to show them.)

Invite each group or pair to choose an article that interests them. Give them five or ten minutes to read the article and then ask them to tell the class broadly what it is about. Make a list of the topics on the board so that learners can see that news reports include a variety of different topics, from national and international news to sport, fashion, music and TV reviews.

Use learners' chosen articles to introduce or review the key features of news reports:

- headline
- journalist's byline
- first summary sentence or paragraph (often in bold type)
- puns or jokes (if appropriate to the subject matter)
- emphatic or engaging language to grab the reader's attention
- quotations from witnesses or people involved in the story
- photographs of a key moment or person in the story.

Invite learners to find as many of these features as possible in their chosen article.

Then introduce learners to the idea that journalists often try to answer the following questions in the first few paragraphs of an article:

- **Who** is the article about?
- **What** happened to them, or what did they do?
- **When** did it happen?
- **Where** did it happen?
- **Why** or **how** did it happen?

Choose a couple of the news reports and, as a whole class, try to identify the answers to these questions.

Ask learners to complete PCM 15 to give them further individual practice in answering these '5W' questions. This also gives you the opportunity to assess whether they have understood the principle.

Unit 6 • Making the headlines

Week 1

Key strands and substrands: Lesson outcomes

Reading

- Read and understand the features of newspaper articles
- Skim to get the gist of a text
- Understand meaning in newspaper articles and identify key words
- Locate information to answer questions
- Make inferences from text
- Use effective strategies to read unfamiliar words
- Record interesting words in spelling logs
- Explore commas in texts
- Identify stressed and unstressed syllables

Writing

- Spell words with silent letters and different vowel sounds
- Generate spelling rules from spelling patterns
- Use effective strategies to spell words correctly

- Use spelling logs of words that need to be learned
- Begin to use commas to make meaning clear
- Make notes on a text to inform writing
- Experiment with varying verb forms

Speaking and listening

- Extend a discussion with comments and questions
- Take turns during a discussion and make links to what others have said

Resources

- Student's Book pages 63–66
- Workbook pages 37–40
- PCM 15: Who, what, when, where, why?
- Slideshows: *Malala's award; New Frog Species Found*
- Audio files: *Malala's award; New Frog Species Found*
- Documentary film about Malala's life: *He called me Malala*

Student's Book pages 63–64

Reading, listening and speaking

1 Tell learners they are going to read a newspaper article. Turn to page 63 and ask learners to skim the article to get an impression of it before they read in detail. Make sure they understand that this means just looking at key features, not reading every word. They should focus on the headline, byline, bold text, photo and caption. Can they work out from these the main topic of the article?

Ask learners to share anything they already know about Malala Yousafzai. Then read the newspaper article aloud to the class, or play the audio recording.

2 Give learners an opportunity to read the text for themselves, and then discuss it in pairs. Circulate as they discuss, so that you can check how well they are listening and responding to each other, and contributing their own ideas. Praise any learners whom you hear dealing politely with an opposing viewpoint (for example, if one partner feels that Malala deserved her Nobel prize and the other does not).

If all of the pairs agree that Malala deserved her prize, you could play 'devil's advocate' and take the opposing view yourself, inviting learners to explain their reasons

for thinking she deserved it. Use this as an opportunity to model courteous ways of dealing with opposing views.

3 Learners can work independently or in pairs to answer the comprehension questions. Many of the questions are open, but even for more closed questions, always allow learners their own variations in the answers, as long as the sense of the answer is correct, and the language used is appropriate.

Answers

3 a Who: Malala Yousafzai. What: received the Nobel Peace Prize. When: she heard about it during a Chemistry lesson at school. Where: Malala originally lived in Pakistan; now she lives in Britain. Why: she received the prize because of her bravery and work campaigning for the right to education.
b It is a summary sentence that gives the reader the gist of the whole article.
c About 57 million.
d She was calm – she decided to go to all her lessons and finish her day at school as usual.
e She is the youngest person/the first young woman ever to receive it.

Unit 6 • Making the headlines

Support: Learners may need further opportunities to practise responding appropriately to opposing viewpoints. You could choose a topic on which you know opinion is divided (such as which is the best football team/rock group, etc.) and ask them to discuss it, modelling polite ways of disagreeing. ('I understand why you might think that, but my opinion is ...', etc.)

Extension: Tackle the following questions with the whole class. Ask learners to look at the first paragraph of the newspaper article on page 63 of the Student's Book.

1 What does this paragraph tell us?

2 Do you think this is an effective opening? Why, or why not?

3 Find two sentences in the article that describe Malala's feelings. Why do you think the writer wanted to include these sentences?

Answers to Extension questions

1 The first paragraph tells us why Malala's work is important and why she was given the prize.

2 It's an open question as to whether learners feel this is an effective opening. On the plus side, it gives very important information about Malala and her award. It also stresses that Malala has worked hard to achieve what she has achieved.

3 Two sentences about Malala's feelings are 'I'm proud I'm the first Pakistani and the first young woman or the first young person who is getting this award. It's a great honour for me.' The writer probably wanted to include these because it makes Malala easier for the reader to identify with, if we know how she felt – we might imagine we would feel a bit like that ourselves, in her position.

Thinking deeper

Have the learners work in groups. Give each group a large sheet of paper. Tell them to read the questions in the Student's Book and then respond to them by writing or drawing on the sheet of paper. They should not discuss the questions, but give personal responses. Then allow time for learners to walk around and read all the responses.

You may want to talk about heroes with the whole class before they begin the activity or you may wish to ask learners what they have learned about heroes after they have read all the other responses.

Workbook page 37
Reading and writing

1–2 Ask learners to complete the activity for homework, using the article on page 63 of the Student's Book. The answers to this activity are open; accept any description that fits with the picture of Malala given in the article.

Workbook page 38
Reading

1–2 If there is time, you could ask learners also to undertake these activities either at home or in class. The activities also link well with later work in this unit, so they can be covered later on if that is preferable.

Student's Book page 65; Workbook page 39
Spelling

1–4 Use the prompts in the Student's Book to review the strategies for spelling multi-syllabic words with the whole class. Learners could work on the activity as a whole class, individually or in pairs. The words in the passage with more than two syllables (excluding names) are: chemistry, another, recognised, promoting, especially, million, recovered, continues, campaigning, decided, considered, organisations, outstanding, achievements, respected.

The rest of the questions are open, depending on the strategies learners choose to use, so it is worth circulating while they work on this activity so that you can check their understanding.

Remind learners that the same phoneme is often spelled in different ways in different words – for example, all these words contain different spellings of the short /u/ sound: 'umbrella', 'young', 'tough', 'mother'. It can be helpful to use spelling journals and lists to group words with different spellings of the same phoneme according to their spellings, and then learn similar words together.

It can also help to group together words where the vowel sound is spelled irregularly after a 'w' – for instance, 'war', 'water', 'work', 'women', 'want'.

1–2 The Workbook spelling activity links with this work. It looks at the spelling of words with common inflections such as –*ing* and –*ed*. These are often multi-syllabic

Unit 6 • Making the headlines

words, but the rules are mostly common to words of any length.

Answers to Workbook questions

1 **a** park   parked, parking
    b dance   danced, dancing
    c try   tried, trying
    d jog   jogged, jogging
    e step   stepped, stepping
    f stamp   stamped, stamping
    g carry   carried, carrying
    h slope   sloped, sloping
    i glide   glided, gliding
    j bury   buried, burying
    k dry   dried, drying
    l change   changed, changing
    m jump   jumped, jumping
    n pin   pinned, pinning

2 **a** walked; **b** hurrying, tripped; **c** placed;
    d lifting; **e** married; **f** voted; **g** knitted; **h** sliding

Student's Book page 66

Punctuation

1–2 Use the prompts in the Student's Book to show learners how commas can be used to separate out part of a sentence that is not essential to the meaning of the whole sentence. (You could introduce the term 'in parenthesis' for these phrases and clauses if you wish, but it isn't essential.) If this is new to learners, it may work well to tackle these questions as a whole class; otherwise, they can complete the questions independently or in pairs.

Answers

1 Malala shares the award with Kailash Satyarthi, **from India**, who has worked for children's rights and against child slavery.
2 **a** Mei's cat, called Fluffy, was extremely fierce.
    b My favourite food is pancakes, especially with chocolate.
    c Kamal's little sister, at the age of only three, won a singing competition.
    d Our next-door neighbour, Mr Fanelli, grows delicious strawberries.
    e I washed the dishes, lots of them, because I wanted to surprise my mother.

Workbook page 40

Punctuation

1–2 Ask learners to complete these activities either as homework or in class.

Answers

1 **a** My dad goes out for a run every morning, often as far as 10-kilometres.
    b I nibbled on some delicious cookies, even though Mum told me not to.
    c Malala, who is from Pakistan, shared the prize with Kailash Satyarthi, from India.
    d Ali, who does not like having a hair cut, has hair dangling in his eyes.
    e It was very cold, almost freezing, so I put on my thick coat.
2 Open question; accept any clauses or phrases that make sense in the context.

Weekly review

Use this rubric to assess learners' progress as they work through the activities this week.
You can use the activities suggested beneath the table to follow up on your on-going assessment.

Level	Reading	Writing	Speaking and listening
■	May need support to read and understand a straightforward newspaper text, especially if it contains unfamiliar language or concepts.[1]	May need further practice to understand the rules and tricks for spelling multi-syllable words and words with common inflections. May need support to understand how commas can be used to separate out part of a sentence that gives extra information.	Needs prompting to listen and respond appropriately in discussion, especially when there are opposing viewpoints.

●	Can understand the gist of a straightforward newspaper article but may need help with aspects that are outside their experience.	Can apply several rules and tricks for spelling multi-syllable words with little support; they may need reminding of other rules. Often able to identify where commas should be used to separate out part of a sentence that gives extra information.	Learning to listen more effectively and respond more appropriately in discussion, and can sometimes think of polite ways of dealing with opposing viewpoints.
▲	Able to read and understand a straightforward newspaper article independently and accurately.[2]	Can apply several rules and tricks for spelling multi-syllable words, and may be able to derive own spelling rules with support. Able to identify where commas should be used to separate out part of a sentence that gives extra information.	Listens effectively and responds appropriately in discussion, and can often think of polite ways of dealing with opposing viewpoints.

Reading[1] Work through PCM 15 again with small groups of learners. Choose one of the articles the class read at the beginning of the week and let them find answers to the five W questions.

Reading[2] Learners can look for interesting news reports online and report back to the class briefly explaining the who, what, when, where and why of the report.

Week 2

Key strands and substrands: Lesson outcomes

Reading
- Read and discuss a newspaper article
- Make inferences from text
- Skim to get an overall sense of a text
- Locate information to answer questions
- Examine a writer's choice of words
- Distinguish between fact and opinion
- Give a personal responses to a text
- Understand meaning in newspaper articles and find key words
- Recognise and comment on puns

Writing
- Plan writing
- Make notes to use in own writing
- Write in a logical sequence, using links, connectives and paragraphs

- Use appropriate features, content and language for newspaper articles
- Explore layout for own writing
- Evaluate own writing, proofread and make corrections
- Adopt a viewpoint in writing

Speaking and listening
- Listen, respond politely and ask questions in discussions
- Contribute to discussions, taking turns

Resources
- Student's Book pages 67–70
- Slideshow: *Mini Mars Mission*
- Audio file: *Mini Mars mission*

Introduction

Explain that learners are going to read, talk about and answer questions on another newspaper article, before they go on to write one of their own. Read the article *Mini Mars mission* to learners, or play the audio recording.

Student's Book pages 67–68

Reading, speaking and writing

1–2 Give learners a chance to read the article independently, and then discuss the questions in the Student's Book in groups or pairs. It may be worth recapping the difference between fact and opinion, before learners start (see Unit 2, page 16). Ask learners why they think a journalist might include opinions as well as facts in a newspaper article. (For example, people interviewed and quoted in the

Unit 6 • Making the headlines

article might express an opinion; or the journalist might state or imply their own opinion. The use of opinions might help to engage the reader and make them think about their own opinion on the subject, and whether they agree with the stated opinions.)

If learners are unfamiliar with spider diagrams (questions 2b and 2c) then discuss with them how this type of graphical organiser can help them to order their thoughts and ideas. A key word is written at the centre of the diagram and other words, ideas and phrases that relate to the key word are added around it. A spider diagram is useful for planning. You could ask learners to write the answers to the questions independently after they discuss them, or you could bring the whole class together to answer the questions orally once the groups or pairs have discussed them.

Answers

2 a Accept any accurate summary, for example: 'A thirteen-year-old girl called Alyssa Carson wants to go to Mars when she grows up, and she is already training to be an astronaut with support from NASA.'

b and c Accept any diagram with words and phrases that describe Alyssa.

d Open question; look for a reasoned explanation of learners' views.

e The puns include 'high hopes', 'out of this world', 'watch this "space"'.

f Learners may feel the puns help to engage the reader's attention and make them smile.

g Look for a reasoned explanation of learners' views.

h Accept any sentences that convey a fact/opinion; example of a sentence with a fact: 'She began training when she was only three years old!' A sentence with an opinion: 'I have made it this far and I don't think I'll be changing my mind.'

i The first planned Mars flight is due in 2033. Alyssa must have been born in about 2001, so she would be about 32 by the time she leaves to go to Mars.

Student's Book pages 69–70

Writing

Planning and writing their own newspaper report should take learners at least two sessions. You may want to guide their choice of person to focus on; for example, you might choose to arrange a visit from an interesting person who lives locally, and ask the whole class to write about them. If some learners do choose to focus on a famous person, it's worth reviewing their choices before they start, to check that appropriate research material is available on websites and/or in books. If their first choice causes problems because of a lack of appropriate material, you can then guide them towards an alternative choice.

Learners can use the prompts in the Student's Book to help them structure the planning, drafting and final writing phase of their article. Circulate among the groups as they work, to check that they understand what to do and to help keep them on track if necessary.

Weekly review

Use this rubric to assess learners' progress as they work through the activities this week. You can use the activities suggested beneath the table to follow up on your on-going assessment.

Level	Reading	Writing	Speaking and listening
■	May need prompting to apply what they learned in the first part of this unit to reading a further newspaper account. However, should be starting to find it easier to identify the key elements of a newspaper report and understand the structure.	Likely to need plenty of support when researching writing a newspaper report. Likely to benefit from a structured/scaffolded approach to the activity.[1]	May need support to stay on track when discussing what they have read

Unit 6 • Making the headlines

●	Getting to know the key features and structure of a newspaper report and can often identify these in reading.	Can work mostly independently to write a newspaper report based on a clear model, though may need some support to include all of the key features of the genre.	Can normally discuss reading sensibly in groups, taking turns and listening to each other.
▲	Reads and understands a range of simple newspaper reports and can talk about the key features and structure.	Can use the key features of a newspaper report effectively to write a simple article, drawing on models they have read and on their own research.[2]	Can work mostly independently to discuss their reading in groups, listening and responding to each other's points courteously.

Writing[1] May benefit from writing collaboratively in a group, rehearsing their sentences orally before writing.

Writing[2] Some learners should be able to research their subject in reasonable depth (asking polite but probing questions if they are interviewing someone, or collecting and noting down useful information from books and websites). They may write an extended article running to several paragraphs. Remind them to make sure that their paragraphs are well organised, so that all the facts about a particular topic are grouped together.

Week 3

Key strands and substrands: Lesson outcomes

Reading

- Read magazine articles, reports and instructions and compare their features
- Make inferences from text
- Understand the structure and features of magazine articles
- Identify and discuss connectives in texts
- Comment on a writer's choice of words
- Understand meaning and find answers in texts
- Compare themes and features of non-fiction texts

Writing

- Use connectives in sentences
- Plan and write a magazine article, using appropriate structure and features
- Write for a specific purpose and audience
- Use punctuation correctly

Resources

- Student's Book pages 71–74
- Workbook page 41
- Slideshows: *Fossil Hunt; Make your own fossil!*
- Audio files: *Fossil Hunt; Make your own fossil!*
- PCM 16: Non-chronological reports
- PCM 17: Instructions

Student's Book pages 71–73

Reading and writing

To introduce this part of the unit on magazine texts, bring in a range of magazines for learners to look at. Magazines about animals, sports and history are often a good choice, as are the weekend magazine supplements included with some newspapers. Distribute the sample magazines and ask learners to note down all the different types of text they can find. Then share their findings as a whole class. Make the point that magazines often contain a very wide range of different types of text, including non-chronological reports, explanations, quizzes, interviews and instructions.

1–2 Give learners time to read 'Fossil Hunt' and 'Make your own fossil!' (or play the audio recording). They can then tackle the comprehension questions individually or in pairs.

Safety note: Do not attempt to make the fossils as described in the 'Make your own fossil' text. The text has been supplied as an example of an instruction text only and should not be treated as a practical activity.

3 Briefly recap learners' earlier work on connectives if necessary, and then use the prompts in the Student's Book to introduce the idea that connectives are used differently in different types of text. You could go through the questions in the

Unit 6 • Making the headlines

Student's Book as a whole class, or ask learners to answer them independently.

Answers

2 a 'Make your own fossil' is an instruction text. Learners may mention various clues, including a bulleted equipment list, numbered instructions and order-style sentences beginning with command verbs for the instructions.
b It has clear headings that pose questions that are answered in the text, with paragraphs grouping similar information together.
c Somewhere where there is sedimentary rock, such as a beach, field or farmland.
d Your eyes
e Fossil hunting can be dangerous, for example if there are rockfalls or a risk of getting cut off by the tide.
f Open question, but for example, three attention-grabbing sentences are: 'Here's what you need to know if you want to be a fossil hunter!', 'If you are very lucky and live in the right place, you might even find a fossil in your garden!' and 'The best bit of kit is your eyes!'
g Open question; learners may mention that the headings help the reader to see what the report is about, and to find the information they need.
h You use it to make the shape of the fossil, by pouring it over modelling clay that has the impression of a toy or shell in it.
i You take the plastic toys out, because you need to pour the plaster into the impression left behind by the toys.
j Most of the sentences are orders; you can tell because there is a command verb at or near the start of the sentence and the sentences address the reader directly.
k Open question; probably because the numbers help the reader to see the order in which things have to be done.
l Open question; learners may mention that the instruction text starts with an attention-grabbing opening aimed at making the reader feel it would be good to make a fossil.
m Open question. Learners may feel that the instructions could be easier to follow if precise instructions were given for using the plaster of Paris, or if there were photos showing each stage of the process.

3 a I went down to the beach (and) jumped straight into the waves.

b (Unfortunately/however/next), I trod on a crab.
c My toe went bright red, (because/as/after/when) the crab nipped it.
d I showed my sister, (but/and) she just laughed at me.
e (However/meanwhile/despite this), when I got home, Mum gave me a plaster for my sore toe.

Extension: If learners need a challenge, ask them to write a list of connectives that are particularly useful when presenting a point of view or an argument, for example, *therefore, however, moreover, because, on the other hand, despite this, so, in conclusion*. Then let them write a couple of paragraphs giving their point of view on an issue of their choice, and to use as many appropriate connectives as possible.

Support: Learners can look for some examples of texts that state an argument or point of view, and find as many connectives as they can in the texts.

Workbook page 41

Reading and writing

1–2 Learners could complete this activity in class or as homework. Ask them to work independently on this, so that you have an opportunity to assess their understanding.

Answers

1 a First, take a paper plate and put the mug or glass down in the middle of it. Draw round the mug or glass so there is a circle in the middle of the plate.
b Next/then cut the circle out of the middle of the plate so you are left with a ring.
c Next/then do the same with three of the other plates.
d Colour or paint the rings using bright colours.
e Finally/next/then, take the cardboard tube and stick it to the last plate with sticky tape, so it will stand upright.
f Now/finally/then throw your rings and see how many you can get to land over the tube!

2 a First take a paper plate and put the mug or glass down in the middle of it. Draw round the mug or glass so there is a circle in the middle of the plate.
b Next/then cut the circle out of the middle of the plate so you are left with a ring.
c Next/then do the same with three of the other plates.

Unit 6 • Making the headlines

d Colour or paint the rings using bright colours.
e Finally/next/then, take the cardboard tube
and stick it to the last plate with sticky tape, so
it will stand upright.
f Now/finally/then throw your rings and see
how many you can get to land over the tube!

Student's Book page 74

Writing

Ask learners to undertake this as an end of unit
review activity. Before they start, remind them about
the structure of non-chronological reports and
instructions. You can use PCMs 16 and 17 as a
focus for this, or ask learners working at a higher
level to look at the examples in the Student's Book
and write their own list of common features in
instructions and reports.

Before learners start planning their pieces, check
that they have chosen a sensible topic (probably
connected to a favourite hobby or sport) and that
they have the necessary resources to research it if
they need to. It may simplify things if you can
organise the class into a few groups who are writing
on similar topics, so that they can share research
and support each other.

Sample learners' work and discussions as they
begin the drafting and writing process, and remind
them to use the stylistic features of reports and
instructions in their own writing (using PCMs 15 and
16 to jog their memories if necessary). Encourage
them to use the checklists in the Student's Book to
make sure that they include all the necessary
elements in their writing.

You could make a class magazine using the
learner's finished pieces, and leave it in the library or
book corner for other classes to browse through.

Support: Simplify this task further for learners who
are struggling with writing. You may ask them to
choose just one piece of writing (for example, the
instructions) rather than two. You could ask them to
use PCM 16 or PCM 17 to structure their writing
(and if you wish, they could actually complete the
writing on a copy of the relevant PCM).

Weekly review

Use this rubric to assess learners' progress as they work through the activities this week. You can use the
activities suggested beneath the table to follow up on your on-going assessment.

Level	Reading	Writing
■	May need support to understand the structure and features of different types of non-fiction writing.[1]	May need support and scaffolding to write a straightforward instruction text and/or non-chronological report.
●	Can identify some key differences between instructions and non-chronological reports, and can work mostly independently to answer straightforward comprehension questions.	Can write and plan a short instruction text and non-chronological report with little support.
▲	Understands the key features and structure of instructions and non-chronological reports, and can work independently to answer comprehension questions on them.	Can accurately use the key features of instruction texts and non-chronological reports in their own writing.[1]

Reading[1] It may help to discuss what learners have read in a group or pair, before answering comprehension
questions. If learners have attempted the answers already, work through the questions again orally and help
them to find the answers in the text.

Writing[1] Learners could write a more extended non-chronological report on their chosen topic, perhaps
including a mock interview or quotes from a famous person, or a quiz for the reader.

Unit 6 • Making the headlines

Task sheet 2

For consolidation and reinforcement, and to assess learners' understanding of the main learning objectives in Units 4, 5 and 6, have learners complete Task sheet 2. Mark and record the task as part of your on-going assessment. See page 6 Assessment in Primary English for guidance.

Marking guidance

Question 1

Reading

A Learner's own words, but they should make the point that it is an attention-grabbing opening and/or that the question makes the reader think about what they are reading. (1)

B Joe Kittinger was the holder of the previous skydiving world record, having jumped from 31 kilometres above Earth, so he had useful experience which would allow him to help Felix. (Or similar sentence in the learner's own words.) (1)

C It was lifted up by a huge helium balloon. (1)

D Accept any two accurate sentences that describe Felix Baumgartner drawing on information from the text, in the learner's own words. (2 – one mark for each sentence)

E Nine minutes. (1)

F Highest BASE jump from a building. (1)

G Accept any clear and accurate sentence that sums up the main point of the report in the learner's own words, for example, 'Felix Baumgartner broke the world record for the highest skydive when he jumped from 39 kilometres above Earth.' (1)

Question 2

Grammar, vocabulary and punctuation

A Statement: accept any sentence from the report that is a statement. Question: 'Have you ever wondered what it would be like to jump from 39 kilometres above the surface of the Earth?' Order: 'Ask Felix Baumgartner – the only human being who has ever tried it.' (3 – one mark for each correct sentence)

B Find out about the champion skydiver Felix Baumgartner.
Tell your friends about Felix's amazing adventure.
(2 – one mark for each correctly rewritten sentence)

C For Felix, the ultimate challenge was to <u>annihilate</u> Colonel Joe Kittinger's record for the highest ever skydive. (beat, smash or a similar verb of the learner's choice)
Less than a minute after <u>evacuating</u> the pod, he had reached his maximum speed of 1,358 kilometres per hour. (leaving, or a similar verb of the learner's choice)
(2 – half a mark for each correct underlining, and half a mark for each alternative verb)

D Felix Baumgartner jumped from an astonishing 39 kilometres above Earth, a record-breaking jump. Felix took a team of experts, lots of equipment and a protective pod to the jump site on 12 October 2012.
(2 – one mark for each correctly punctuated sentence.)

Question 3

Writing

A 10 marks – allow one mark for each of five sentences, and one mark for fulfilling each of these criteria:
- a headline
- a punchy opening
- the key facts
- the learner's own opinion of what Felix did
- at least two sentences with powerful verbs.

Unit 7 Inventions

Unit overview

This unit looks at two different types of non-fiction texts: alphabetically organised encyclopedias and explanations. Learners will read extracts from an encyclopedia about inventions, and explanations about how some of the inventions work. They will answer comprehension questions and practise writing their own encyclopedia entries and explanations, based on the model texts they have read. They will also write a letter to a newspaper putting forward their own point of view and giving reasons. The unit also includes a poem on the subject of inventions, and offers opportunities to explore alphabetical order, revise end-of-sentence punctuation and look at past, present and future tenses in a range of different types of sentence.

Introducing the unit

Bring in a range of reference texts for learners to look at – including dictionaries, encyclopedias and other clearly organised reference books. You could also give access to searchable reference websites, such as the Natural History Museum website (nhm.ac.uk).

Give each group or pair different types of reference texts, and tell them that they have ten minutes to look at how their texts are organised, and what a reader might use them for. Ask them to make brief notes about this so that they can feed back to the rest of the class.

Share learners' thoughts about their reference texts. Look in particular at how these texts are organised. For example, many reference texts use alphabetical ordering; others use clear headings that are grouped thematically so that the reader can easily find particular information. Historical texts are often organised chronologically. Talk about how it's particularly important for a reference text to be clearly organised, since this helps the reader to find specific information.

Spend some time looking at how illustrations are used in the reference texts, and identifying what extra information they add to the text.

Ask each group or pair to think of at least one question that can be answered using one of their reference texts. Then swap texts and questions with another group, and find out the answer to the other group's question.

Unit 7 • Inventions

Week 1

Key strands and substrands: Lesson outcomes

Reading

- Read and recognise the key features of alphabetically organised texts
- Understand meaning and identify key words and phrases
- Locate information to answer questions
- Organise words alphabetically
- Explore and recognise how ideas are organised and points sequenced
- Discuss and compare purposes and feature of texts
- Locate books by classification

Writing

- Make notes and use them in writing
- Write for a specific purpose and audience
- State own viewpoint
- Write in a logical sequence using connectives

- Organise writing in paragraphs with appropriate organisational features
- Evaluate and proofread own writing

Speaking and listening

- Speak accurately with precise vocabulary, showing awareness of audience
- Listen, respond and contribute ideas in a discussion
- Respond politely and take turns in a discussion

Resources

- Student's Book pages 75–79
- Workbook pages 42–44
- Slideshow: *Encyclopedia of Inventions*
- Audio file: *Encyclopedia of Inventions*
- PCM 18: Letter to a newspaper
- PCM 19: Write a friendly letter
- PCM 20: Write a formal letter

Student's Book pages 75–78

Reading and writing

1 Learners can read the extract from *An Encyclopedia of Inventions* either silently to themselves, or out loud in a group or pair. You may wish to play the audio recording through once before learners do this. Circulate while they are reading so that you can answer any questions or explain words they do not know.

2 Learners can then answer the comprehension questions individually or in pairs. Many of the questions are open, but even for more closed questions, always allow learners their own variations in the answers, as long as the sense of the answer is correct, and the language used is appropriate.

Answers
2 a 1938
   b It was cleaner because there was less risk of spilling ink; it was also quicker and more convenient.
   c It was made of wood, and it had no pedals.
   d 1913
   e John Montagu, Earl of Sandwich, because he created the first sandwich.

f Open question, but key words and phrases include: 'said to have been invented by … John Montagu', 'didn't want to stop for a proper meal', 'meat between two slices of bread'.
g Answer should be along the lines of 'John Montagu invented the sandwich because he didn't want to stop playing cards and eat a proper meal'.
h leather
i Cardigan and Wellington boot
j They keep the windscreen clear of rainwater, so the driver can see properly.
k Alphabetically by name of invention.
l aeroplane
   ballpoint pen
   battery
   bicycle
   cardigan
   central heating
   computer
   fridge
   light bulb
   microwave
   sandwich
   scooter
   telephone

Unit 7 • Inventions

washing machine
wellington boot
wheelchair
windscreen wiper

Alphabetical order

3 If learners are not familiar with the idea of using more than one letter in a word to work out alphabetical order, use the 'Alphabetical order' box to introduce this idea. It can help to write the words on separate slips of paper, so that learners can experiment with putting them in order, and only write the words as a list once they are sure.

Extension: Learners can complete the 'Alphabetical order' activity independently, and they may also be able to create their own alphabetic list (perhaps related to a favourite hobby) using up to the first four or five letters of some words to determine the correct order.

Support: Learners may need further opportunities to practise ordering words alphabetically. If they are struggling, give them a list of words that can be ordered using the first letter of each word alone, and make sure they have access to a chart or list showing alphabetical order. Once they are confident in ordering words alphabetically using the first letter, introduce some words where they need to look at the second letter, and so on.

Answers
3 badminton, baseball, basketball, cricket, football, rounders, rugby, squash, table tennis, tennis, volleyball

Workbook pages 42–43
Spelling

1–3 The Workbook activities on alphabetical order provide extra practice, and can be completed in class or as homework.

Answers
1 anteater; antelope; elephant; elk; hare; hippopotamus; kangaroo; koala; lion; lizard; mouse; rabbit
2 Bains; Burroughs; Howard; Hussain; Khan; Latimer; Lau; Patel; Persaud; Peters; Smithson; Wang

3 Check that learners have put their chosen names in the correct alphabetical order from left to right.

Student's Book pages 78–79
Listening and speaking

1–3 Circulate while learners discuss the prompts in the Student's Book in their pairs or groups. Some groups may need help to remember to listen to each other's views and respond courteously to others who don't agree with them. You could model this for them if necessary, by suggesting an alternative, politer way of responding. Remind learners to make notes so they can remember their key reasons for deciding on the most and least important inventions. Encourage them to practise explaining their reasons so that they are able to do so concisely when presenting their group's views to the rest of the class.

If you wish, you could have a vote to find the most popular and least popular invention.

Workbook page 44
Reading and writing

1–6 Before learners turn their notes from the speaking and listening activity into a letter explaining their views, you may wish to give them PCM 18, which includes a helpful model of a letter to a newspaper, and ask them to complete the Workbook activity. Alternatively, this activity can be done later, either in class or as homework.

Answers
1 The internet helps people to stay connected, even if they live far apart; it contains useful information; it is a source of entertainment; it is convenient for shopping.
2 It helps people who live far apart to stay in touch.
3 6 January
4 Open question; look for at least one reason to explain the learner's opinion.
5 Open question; look for a clear explanation and at least two supporting reasons.
6 Any three connectives from: first of all; so; but; also; secondly; if; in addition; when; and; in conclusion

Unit 7 • Inventions

Student's Book page 79

Writing

1–3 Learners can use the prompts in the Student's Book, along with their notes, to help them structure their own letter. Encourage them to use the bulleted lists at first draft stage, so they can check they have included all the necessary information and features.

Extension: Learners should be able to write a letter that presents their argument in an ordered way, working mostly independently. However, it may be useful to review their work at draft stage so that you can prompt them to make any necessary changes.

Weekly review

Use this rubric to assess learners' progress as they work through the activities this week. You can use the activities suggested beneath the table to follow up on your on-going assessment.

Level	Reading	Writing	Speaking and listening
■	Needs support to read and use an alphabetically organised reference text.	Needs support when writing a letter that explains their views.[1]	Needs prompting to listen and respond appropriately in discussion, especially when there are opposing viewpoints.
●	Can understand a simple alphabetically organised reference text and is able to work mostly independently, with some support from the teacher as necessary.	Needs some support initially when writing a letter that explains their views, but is able to finish the task fairly independently.[1]	Learning to listen more effectively and respond more appropriately in discussion, and can sometimes think of polite ways of dealing with opposing viewpoints.
▲	Is able to read and understand an alphabetically organised reference text independently and accurately.	Can work independently to write a letter that explains views, using an existing letter as a model if necessary.	Listens effectively and responds appropriately in discussion, and can often think of polite ways of dealing with opposing viewpoints.

Writing[1] Learners may benefit from using a letter writing frame on PCM 19 or PCM 20 to help them structure their letter. They may also work in pairs or groups, discussing the letter as they write. You can support them by checking their work at each stage, and discussing what they need to do so that they understand. Their final draft could be a collaborative effort or written individually, as you prefer.

Unit 7 • Inventions

Week 2

Key strands and substrands: Lesson outcomes

Reading

- Read and explore poems
- Understand explicit and implicit meaning, and make inferences
- Locate information to answer questions
- Understand how verbs tenses are used in texts
- Discuss and compare purposes and feature of texts

Writing

- Use past, present and future verb forms accurately
- Use accurate end-of-sentence punctuation
- Punctuate direct speech
- Make short notes to inform writing
- Explore ways of planning writing

- Write for a specific purpose and audience
- Organise writing in paragraphs and sections or with bullets and numbers
- Write legibly and check writing for grammar, spelling and punctuation

Speaking and listening

- Listen and respond appropriately, asking questions
- Sequence relevant information to aid understanding
- Speak accurately with precise vocabulary

Resources

- Student's Book pages 80–83
- Workbook page 45–46
- Slideshows: *A Good Idea; I'm bored with walking to school*
- Audio files: *A Good Idea; I'm bored with walking to school*

Introduction

Explain to learners that this week they are going to read and think about a poem about an invention, and then they will design and write about a new invention of their own.

Student's Book pages 80–81

Reading and writing

1 Play the audio recording of the poem to learners, or read it aloud to them. Then ask them to read it through out loud in their pairs, taking one role (inventor or questioner) each. If possible, give the pairs time to practise and perfect their reading, adding suitable expression and emphasis, and maybe also developing some actions to go with the poem. The pairs could then take turns to perform the poem for the class.

2 You could ask learners to write the answers to the questions independently, or to discuss them first in their pairs or groups.

Answers

2 a Look for a good description of the invention in the learner's own words. The description should cover the key facts: the invention is to help Mum get the dinner ready, and it has

different arms that do different things including stirring gravy, peeling and chopping potatoes, and going to the shop to buy potatoes.

b The greengrocer's

c There is money in the basket, so the greengrocer can take out the money and put in the potatoes.

d In case someone tries to steal the money.

e To help Mum/so that Mum can have time off.

f Because the invention won't be ready in time for dinner (if ever!).

g Accept any question and answer from the poem.

h The speakers are the inventor and someone else, who could be a friend or a family member (though not Mum).

i Learners should spot that the start of the poem says 'I might just make one of my inventions' – this suggests that the inventor has made inventions before.

j Look for good clear reasons for the learner's view.

© HarperCollins*Publishers* 2021

Unit 7 • Inventions

Student's Book page 81

Using verb tenses

1–2 Learners could complete these questions independently, or you may prefer to discuss the questions as a whole class and complete them orally.

Answers

1 Accept any sentences from the poem that are in the present and the future.
2 **a** I will go into town with Mara and Jake.
 b Dad is cross with us.
 c Uncle Ike will make lamb curry for dinner.
 d My favourite TV show was *Dinosaur Wars*.
 e It will be bedtime when we get to Gran's house.
 f Jamie is running home because it is raining.

Workbook page 45

Verb tenses

1–4 Learners can complete these activities independently, in class or for homework.

Support: Learners may benefit from working together as a group to answer these questions, with teacher support as needed.

Answers

1 **a** Orla won the running race.
 b I was glad to see Ella.
2 **a** We will go to the beach on Saturday.
 b They will paint Grace's bedroom pink.
3 **a** Janine sees the three kittens.
 b Mum is going to the shops. (or 'Mum goes')
4 It was Saturday afternoon, and I was bored. Well, can you blame me? Nothing interesting will ever happen in our house. I had played all my games and read all my books, and I had nothing to do.
 Suddenly, there was a knock on my bedroom door. I got a shock!
 "Who is that? What do you want?"
 I crept to the door and opened it. You will never guess what I saw!

Student's Book page 82

Punctuation

1–2 Encourage learners to read through the poem in their pairs before they add the missing punctuation – this will help them work out which sentences are questions or exclamations, and which are simple statements.

Answers

1 I'm bored with walking to school.
 Today I'm going to fly there!
 But where are your wings?
 Here they are, in my bag.
 They're a bit crumpled,
 but they're not broken.
 How do they work?
 I just pull this string
 and jump up into the air
 as high as I can.
 Then I make a wish and –
 look – I can fly!
2 Learners' own responses

Workbook page 46

Punctuation

1–2 Learners can complete these activities independently.

Answers

1 **a** I'm so glad you're coming round to our house to play!
 b Do you like chocolate?
 c It's my dad's birthday on Wednesday.
 d My teacher's name is Mrs Ismael.
 e There's a wasp on your arm!
 f I've never felt so happy!
 g There's a dragon in the playground!
 h How many sisters do you have?
 i Dad's favourite colour is green.
 j On Saturday we went to the shops.
2 Accept any accurately punctuated sentences that fit the brief.

Student's Book page 83

Listening and speaking

1–3 Ask learners to use the prompts in the Student's Book to help structure their discussion about their inventions. If any learners struggle to think of an idea for an invention, prompt them to think about their favourite hobby or activity – what could they invent that would help them with this?

Circulate among the groups so that you can make sure they are discussing the inventions constructively. Remind them to make notes of their ideas, so that they can use these in the writing activity that follows.

Writing

1–5 The notes in the Student's Book, page 83, can be used to structure the writing activity. Encourage learners to reread the *Encyclopedia of Inventions* to help them structure their pieces in a similar way.

Some learners will need support as they work. Check that they go through all the suggested stages as they write.

When learners have written their pieces, review them as a whole class. Make a list of the inventions and ask learners to order the list alphabetically. Then you can make an alphabetically organised class *Encyclopedia of Inventions*!

Weekly review

Use this rubric to assess learners' progress as they work through the activities this week. You can use the activities suggested beneath the table to follow up on your on-going assessment.

Level	Reading	Writing	Speaking and listening
■	Needs help to answer questions about poems.[1]	Needs support to write a short encyclopedia entry based on a clear model text.	Needs extra practice and support to read a poem out loud with appropriate expression and actions.
●	Able to answer most questions about poems in pairs.	Can work mostly independently to write a short encyclopedia entry based on a model text.	After practising, is able to understand how to read a poem aloud with some appropriate expression, intonation and actions.[1]
▲	Able to work independently or in pairs to read and answer questions about poems.	Can confidently use most of the features of a short encyclopedia entry in their own writing, with minimal support.	Able to develop a performance of a poem with appropriate expression, intonation and actions, working mostly independently.

Reading[1] Read the poem again and work through the questions with small groups of learners.
Speaking and listening[1] Let learners listen to the audio recording of the poem they have performed and discuss what else they could do to improve their own performance. Then let them try again.

Week 3

Key strands and substrands: Lesson outcomes

Reading

- Suggest synonyms for words in texts
- Compare the features of non-fiction texts
- Explore words with common roots
- Explore and recognise how ideas are organised and points sequenced
- Discuss and compare purposes and feature of texts
- Express personal responses to a text

Writing

- Write an explanation, using appropriate language and features
- Spell words with prefixes and suffixes and explore words with related roots

- Plan writing
- Use specialised vocabulary
- Develop a sequence of ideas, using paragraphs and appropriate organisational features
- Evaluate and proofread own work

Resources

- Student's Book pages 84–86
- Workbook pages 47–48
- Slideshow: *How do zips work?*
- Audio file: *How do zips work?*

Unit 7 • Inventions

Student's Book page 84

Reading and writing

1–3 Give learners time to read *How do zips work?* (or play the audio recording). They can then tackle the comprehension questions individually or in pairs.

Answers

3 **a** Open question; answers along the lines of 'The teeth of a zip are the metal bits that stick out on either side of the zip and lock together when the slider is pulled.'

b Ingenious

c It forces the teeth on either side of the zip together (to close the zip) or apart (to open the zip).

d Open question; perhaps in order to separate out the information clearly and make it easier to read and follow.

e The present tense. Open question; perhaps because the text is describing something that is happening (or could be happening) in the present, not just in the past or future.

f Open question; perhaps because diagrams can help to convey a complex process more clearly than words alone.

Student's Book page 85
Writing

1–2 This short writing activity provides useful practice for the longer writing activity that concludes this unit.

Use the prompts in the Student's Book to structure this activity, and circulate as learners work on their explanations, in pairs or individually. You could introduce the task by discussing what learners have to do as a whole class, and talking about the information that the diagram gives us. You could model how to turn this information from the diagram into a few sentences of continuous text.

Extension: Learners should be able to write a brief explanation text modelled on the one about zips, using just the information from the Student's Book.

Support: Learners may benefit from working collaboratively on this task, and you may want to work with them so that you can make sure they understand what they need to do.

Spelling

1–2 Introduce these activities by reminding learners about their previous work on word families and words based on a common root. Explain that when we make a noun from a verb, the noun normally ends in 'ion' or 'ment'. You could do Spelling activity 1 as a whole class.

Answers

1 invent; act; imagine; move; judge

2 open question

Thinking deeper

Make a set of word cards with the following words: enjoy, agree, invent, create, instruct, educate, express.

Give each team a set of word cards. Learners take turns to choose a word and make a noun in the same word family by adding an ending. Each learner has 30 seconds to make and spell the word correctly.

Answers

enjoy – enjoyment; agree – agreement; invent – invention; create – creation; instruct – instruction; educate – education; express – expression

Workbook pages 47–48
Spelling

1–4 Learners can complete these activities either in class or as homework.

Use this work as an opportunity to revise spelling patterns for adding other common suffixes and inflections, as well as *–ment* and *–ion*; for example *–ing*, *–ed* and *–s*.

Answers

1 excitement, celebration, management, connection, agreement, decision, definition, argument, diversion, measurement, education, operation

operate, decide, divert, excite, define, celebrate, manage, educate, measure, connect, agree, argue

Unit 7 • Inventions

2 **a** announce; **b** contradict; **c** punish;
   d demonstrate; **e** entertain; **f** co-operate;
   g encourage

3 **a** decoration; **b** possession; **c** assessment;
   d navigation; **e** payment; **f** irritation;
   g announcement

4 The nine letter word is operation; check
   learners' answers for other words.

Student's Book page 86

Writing

Ask learners to undertake this activity as an end of unit review activity. Encourage them to use the short explanation text that they wrote about ballpoint pens as a model for this piece of work. (It may be worth displaying one or two good examples from the class on the wall, so that learners who have not produced a clear model themselves, can use them to help structure their work.)

Encourage learners to rehearse their explanations orally before they start to write; explaining things orally is a good preparation for writing. Listen in to the pairs' verbal explanations as they do this, and prompt them to include any aspects of the explanation that they may have forgotten.

Check that learners make clear notes under the headings suggested, and that they use these notes to help them structure their final text. Encourage learners to use the prompts in the Student's Book when they check their work.

Thinking time

Allow time for learners to reflect on whether they found it easy or difficult to write an explanation of how something works.

Weekly review

Use this rubric to assess learners' progress as they work through the activities this week. You can use the activities suggested beneath the table to follow up on your on-going assessment.

Level	Reading	Writing
■	Needs support to understand the structure and features of explanation texts and other reference texts.	Needs support and scaffolding to write a straightforward explanation text.[1]
●	Can identify some key features of explanation texts and other reference texts, and is beginning to understand how these texts work.	Can write and plan a short explanation text with little support.
▲	Understands the key features and structure of explanation texts and other reference texts, and can replicate many of these in their own writing.	Can accurately use the key features of explanation texts to help them write an interesting and comprehensible explanation.[2]

Writing[1] Prepare a sheet to help learners structure their explanation, with the headings suggested in the Student's Book and with space to write under each heading.

Writing[2] Learners could write an additional explanation text based on the invention that they made up earlier in the unit. Can they explain clearly how their invention would work, and draw a diagram to go with this?

Unit 8 Putting on a show

Unit overview

In this unit, learners will listen to a summary of the story of *Peter and the Wolf* and then read a playscript version of the musical story. They will also read and compare a diary entry and a playscript about a real-life event. They will explore the common features of playscripts, answer comprehension questions and have a go at writing their own mini-plays. They will act out their plays and explore various drama activities in role. They will look at powerful verbs and adverbs, and will practise spelling plural forms of nouns. They will also revise alphabetical order, and apply it when using dictionaries.

Introducing the unit

Explain to learners that they will be reading and acting out some playscripts. Share any experience of plays learners may have seen or performed in themselves. Talk about some of the differences between playscripts and stories:

- Stories often describe things in detail; playscripts tend to concentrate on the words the characters say.
- Stories use direct speech, punctuated with speech marks, and so on; playscripts have the characters' names in the margin followed by the words they say, without speech marks.
- Instead of long descriptive passages or details of how characters think and feel, playscripts have stage directions to tell the actors how to move and speak their lines.
- In stories, the author can describe what is happening and give the reader information about things that might be happening in different times and places; in playscripts, the plot is driven by the words the characters say, almost as if the audience were there with them in real time.
- Playscripts are organised in sections, called acts and scenes. Stories are organised in chapters.

Week 1

Key strands and substrands: Lesson outcomes

Reading

- Read and explore the features of a playscript
- Understand the main ideas and meaning in a text, and make inference
- Understand how characters and setting are developed
- Predict events in a text
- Recognise and compare the features of different texts
- Understand verb tenses in texts
- Identify powerful verbs

Writing

- Write character profiles
- Use verb tenses accurately and vary verb forms
- Use adverbs

Speaking and listening

- Listen and respond appropriately
- Extend a discussion by contributing comments
- Portray a character through speech, gesture and movement

Resources

- Student's Book pages 87–90
- Workbook page 49
- Slideshows: *Peter and the Wolf* (summary); *Peter and the Wolf*
- Audio files: *Peter and the Wolf* (summary); *Peter and the Wolf*
- PCM 21: *Peter and the Wolf:* story summary
- Recording of Prokofiev's Peter *and the Wolf*, if available

---

Unit 8 • Putting on a show

Student's Book page 87

Listening and speaking

1 Tell learners that the first playscript they will look at is based on the story of *Peter and the Wolf* by Prokofiev. If possible, play a recording of *Peter and the Wolf* or a video of a live performance of the story to the class so that they can enjoy the music and begin to get a sense of the story.

Then read the short summary of the plot of Peter and the Wolf aloud to learners, or play the audio. The text of the summary is on PCM 21. Explain to learners that while they listen to the summary, they should make some quick notes to help them remember the main points of the story.

2–3 When learners have listened to the summary at least once, ask them to take turns to retell the story to their partners. Circulate and listen to the retellings so that you can assess how well learners are able to summarise and retell the story.

Extension: Encourage learners who are able to retell the story accurately to think of ways of making their retelling more interesting. For example, the story summary doesn't include any dialogue. Can they make up some words for the characters to say in their retelling?

Tell them that they should not just read the summary out – you want them to annotate it and find the key words and phrases that will help them retell each part of the story. Then they can use these key words in their retelling.

Support: If necessary, model for learners how to role-play the interview between the wolf and the TV reporter. Encourage learners playing the wolf to think about how the wolf might feel about the end of the story, and what he might do in the future.

If you would like to give learners more practice at retelling a story concisely, give them some picture books and ask them to read the story and then retell it. They can note down the main things that happen and some key words to help them retell each incident.

You could use this as an opportunity to explore different ways of saying similar things. For instance, maybe in one pair's interview, the wolf feels very bitter towards Peter and is planning to escape from the zoo and get his revenge. This wolf might express himself very angrily. The wolf in another pair's interview might be more relaxed about it; perhaps still cross with Peter, but feeling that life in the zoo won't be so bad. Learners could look at different ways of expressing these thoughts, and compare the sort of language used in each.

Student's Book pages 88–90

Reading and writing

Before reading, go through some of the features of playscripts with the class briefly. Talk about the layout of the playscript and make sure learners know where to look for information: the names of the characters, the setting for each scene and the stage directions. Ask a few pre-reading questions such as: 'Into how many sections is this extract from the play divided? Where does the first scene take place?'

1–2 Ask learners to read the playscript carefully before they answer the questions. It would be very helpful if learners have the opportunity to read the playscript aloud in a group of eight (or a group of four, doubling up parts). If time allows, encourage them to add movement to their reading, and to use their voices as expressively as possible. If necessary, remind them not to read the stage directions (in brackets) out loud, but silently. They can use the information in the stage directions to help them act out their role expressively.

> *Answers*
>
> **2 a** Because Grandfather knew that a wolf lived in the forest, and he thought Peter would be in danger if he played in the meadow.
>
> **b** He is sent to his room.
>
> **c** Duck.
>
> **d** To make a lasso to trap the wolf by his tail.
>
> **e** Flies round and round the wolf's head until he is dizzy.
>
> **f** Because he knows that Peter has been very brave.
>
> **g** Open question; learners should realise that these are stage directions, and they help the actor understand how to move and how to say the lines.
>
> **h** The words in capitals need to be spoken loudly and with lots of emphasis.
>
> **i** Open question; look for responses that describe Peter accurately, including information about what he looks like, what he does and what kind of person he is.
>
> **j** Open question; accept any sensible answer that fits with the text.

Unit 8 • Putting on a show

Extension: Have a class discussion about the differences between playscripts and stories.

Ask the following questions:

1 How many differences can you think of between the way stories are written and the way plays are written?

2 Think of at least three ways in which playscripts make it easier for the actors to see what they need to do.

Learners' answers to question 1 should include:

- Playscripts are laid out differently from stories, with the speaker's name in the margin and no speech marks.
- Playscripts use stage directions to describe what is going on, to help the actors act out the scene. Stories often use narration to describe what is going on, and sometimes stories tell us about things that can't be seen or heard (which is less common in plays).

In answer to question 2, the ways in which playscripts make it easier for actors to see what they have to do include:

- setting out the speeches clearly on separate lines
- putting the name of the speaker in the margin so actors can just glance down the margin to find their character's next speech
- putting stage directions in italics so they look different from the words the actors speak
- describing how the actor should move and speak in the stage directions.

Thinking deeper

Learners work in groups. They choose one scene from *Peter and the Wolf*. Let one learner in the group volunteer to say what happens in this scene (as a storyteller would). Then have the groups read the playscript aloud. Let them use these experiences as a basis for discussing the questions in the Student's Book. The learners' answers will be their personal opinions, but prompt them to talk about the way that the characters are created and can come to life through dialogue (and props/costumes sometimes) in a play.

Student's Book page 90

Using verb tenses

1–5 Learners could complete these activities in pairs, or you may prefer to tackle them as a whole class.

Answers

1 creeping, prowls, jumping, ran, waddled, tried to run, runs, catches up, climbed, ran, scrambles, fly, flying, plodded, skipped

2 Open question; look for actions that show the learner has understood the meaning of the word, and clarify if necessary.

3 creeping (present), prowls (present), jumping (present), ran (past), waddled (past), tried to run (past), runs (present), catches up (present), climbed (past), scrambles (present), fly (present), flying (present), plodded (past), skipped (past)

4 The present tense; learners should realise that this is because the characters are talking about the action as it happens, and therefore they are using the present tense.

5 Open question, but learners should notice that the Narrator is telling the story as if it were something that had already happened, so the past tense is appropriate.

Workbook page 49

Verbs and adverbs

1–2 Learners could tackle these activities either in class or as homework. They can also be done later in the unit, if you prefer.

Answers

1 a Li-Wei stomped crossly out of the room.
   b Maxine grabbed the plate and hurled it out of the window.
   c "How dare you do that?" Mum thundered.
   d Romy's cat, Alexia, slunk in through the door.
   e "It wasn't my fault," muttered Sam.
   f The hippopotamus wallowed in the soft river mud.
   g Eight pigeons strutted towards us, looking for food.
   h I yelled at my brother because he used my pens without asking.

2 Open; accept any answers that use the correct adverbs.

Unit 8 • Putting on a show

Weekly review

Use this rubric to assess learners' progress as they work through the activities this week. You can use the activities suggested beneath the table to follow up on your on-going assessment.

Level	Reading	Writing	Speaking and listening
■	Needs support to compare features of playscripts and stories.[1]	Needs to be prompted and/or supported to listen attentively and write short notes to remind them of the key events in a story.[1]	Struggles to read a playscript fluently out loud; may need several readings to become confident enough with the text to start adding expression and actions. Struggles to improvise a new scene.
●	Understands and can describe basic features of playscripts and can compare with stories.	Listens to a story with some attention, and takes notes to help remember at least some parts of the story.	Able to read a playscript with some accuracy, and some use of appropriate expression, after one or two readings Can improvise and act out a short scene that links in some ways to a scene they have read.
▲	Understands and can describe features of playscripts and stories and can compare them.	Can write appropriate notes as they listen to a story, noting only the most important parts of the story.	Can read a playscript with accuracy and fluency and appropriate expression, often on the first reading. Improvises an interesting short scene that links to what they have read.

Reading[1] Compile a table on the board or on a poster with the class on which you show points of comparison between a playscript and story.

Writing[1] Work with small groups of learners and read them a familiar story. They can note down the main things that happen and some key words to help them retell each incident.

Unit 8 • Putting on a show

Week 2

Key strands and substrands: Lesson outcomes

Reading

- Read and compare a diary entry and a playscript
- Use knowledge of punctuation and grammar to read with understanding
- Explore explicit and implicit meanings and make inferences
- Identify figurative language
- Understand the key features and purposes of playscripts and diaries
- Record interesting words in spelling logs
- Suggest synonyms

Writing

- Write a playscript, using appropriate layout and features
- Evaluate others' writing
- Create and use spelling rules for plurals and words with prefixes
- Create and use spelling strategies

- Express viewpoint

Speaking and listening

- Plan a group presentation, taking assigned roles
- Discuss how meaning can be expressed non-verbally
- Listen, respond, and ask and answer questions
- Portray character by adapting speech, gesture and movement
- Evaluate own and other's talk
- Use non-verbal communication techniques

Resources

- Student's Book pages 91–95
- Workbook pages 50–51
- Slideshows: *Zlata's Diary*; *Zlata's Diary* (playscript)
- Audio files: *Zlata's Diary*; *Zlata's Diary* (playscript)
- PCM 22: A difficult decision: character cards

Introduction

Explain that learners are going to read and compare a diary entry and a playscript. Remind them about the diary entry they read in Unit 1, and briefly recap the features of diaries (e.g. they are in the first person, have a date, may be addressed to 'Dear Diary', talk about what the writer has done, seen or felt). Ask learners to read the pieces silently to themselves; they can then discuss the comprehension questions in pairs before they go on to write the answers.

Student's Book pages 91–92

Reading and writing

Explain to the class that Zlata Filipovic wrote the diary extract in the middle of a war. Let learners find out where Sarajevo is on a map. Learners can also find out more about Zlata Filipovic by doing a search on the internet to find out what she is doing now.

1–3 Learners should work in pairs to read the diary entry and the playscript and then discuss and answer the questions.

Answers

2 a Behind the built-in bookcase
   b Because there's a war on (and we infer that it would be dangerous to leave the house).
   c The cat
   d She helped take all the books off the bookcase.
   e 'Waiting ready to pounce'; 'very upset/nervous'; 'feeling she is going mad'

3 a Accept any four (or more) reasonable differences between diary and playscript. These could include: the diary is written in narrative, like a story, whereas the playscript is mostly dialogue; the diary tells us how the characters felt but not what they said; the playscript gives their words and (in stage directions) describes how they spoke and moved); the playscript uses character names in the margin to show who is speaking; the playscript does not talk about what might happen next or give Zlata's ideas about what is happening; the diary is written like a letter to a friend, but the playscript is more like a report of a conversation.

© HarperCollins*Publishers* 2021

Unit 8 • Putting on a show

b Learners might mention that the playscript shows Mummy's actual words and makes it very clear what she has to do in order to show how she is feeling.

Student's Book page 93

Writing

1 Use the Student's Book activity to check that learners have understood how to convert a story into a playscript. Learners will need to think about what the characters might say to each other, because this is not included in the diary. It can be helpful to work through the beginning of the scene together as a whole class, and model how to think about what the characters might say – you can make suggestions and ask learners to contribute their ideas too, before writing their own playscripts.

Learners who find this activity difficult could work in groups, and go through the lines orally before writing them down.

2 Give all the groups time to act out their playscript before moving on. This will help them get into role as the story characters when they attempt the role play.

Student's Book pages 93–94

Listening and speaking

1–3 Use the Student's Book prompts to structure this role-play activity. Allow plenty of time for learners to think about 'their' character's likely response before they start acting it out. It could be helpful if you can circulate at this point and make sure that all learners are in role. If not, refocus them on their characters and think together about how the characters might react.

When the groups have finished their role-play, give them time to evaluate it and practise again, making any changes they need to. Then encourage some or all the groups to show their scene to the whole class.

Extension: Learners can be encouraged to record their conversation in playscript format.

Support: Learners may benefit from having several goes at the conversation, especially if they find it hard to stay in role as their given character. Groups that struggle to understand their characters' motivation could be given PCM 22 which contains prompt cards for each character to get the conversation started. (You could give these cards to all groups if you wish.)

Student's Book pages 94–95

Spelling

1–3 Use the prompts in the Student's Book to teach the rules for spelling words with the prefixes *in–*, *im–*, *il–* and *ir–*, and for making singular nouns plural.

Reinforce this and any other current spelling work by dictating some sentences for learners to write down. This will enable you to assess whether learners can identify the correct spelling pattern for a particular word aurally.

Read these aloud to learners twice, speaking slowly and clearly, and give learners time to write each sentence down before moving on to the next one. When they have finished, collect their sentences in so that you can assess how accurately they were able to spell the target words. If they struggle to remember the whole sentence for long enough to write it, do some more practice, beginning with shorter sentences and working up to longer ones.

Answers
1. inhuman; illogical; immortal; insane; impolite; inconvenient; irrational; inaudible
2. cats; books; shelves; bushes; elves; babies; watches; ladies; boxes; flies; messes; telephones
3. Look for sentences that are correctly spelled and show an understanding of the meaning of the target words.

Workbook page 50

Spelling

1–2 Learners can also complete these activities either in class or as homework.

Answers
1. invisible
   illogical
   incredible
   impossible
   irrelevant
   immature
   incorrect
2. Down
   1. invisible
   2. impossible
   3. incorrect
   4. incredible

Unit 8 • Putting on a show

Across
4 irrelevant
5 illogical
6 immature

Workbook page 51

Spelling

Learners can complete this activity either in class or as homework.

Answers
a shelves; **b** branches; **c** wolves; **d** diaries;
e characters

Vocabulary

1 Learners can also complete activity 1 in class or as homework.

Answers
1 **a** sing (*or* tweet, twitter, peep, and so on)
  b staggered (*or* walked, swayed, and so on)
  c danced (*or* ran, hopped, jumped, and so on)
  d cross (*or* furious, mad, and so on)
  e hung (*or* dropped, swung, and so on)

Weekly review

Use this rubric to assess learners' progress as they work through the activities this week. You can use the activities suggested beneath the table to follow up on your on-going assessment.

Level	Reading	Writing	Speaking and listening
■	Needs support to understand and identify the differences between the way a story is written and the way a playscript is written.	Needs extra structure and support when changing a story into a playscript; they will benefit from lots of practice.	Needs support to work on a simple, structured role-play in a group.[1]
●	Has a good understanding of some of the differences between stories and playscripts.	Can convert a simple story into a playscript mostly accurately, and may include some stage directions derived from the story text.	Can work mostly independently on a group role-play. May sometimes lapse out of character.
▲	Understands the main differences between stories and playscripts and can also identify some more subtle differences related to the way playscripts are used.	Can convert a simple story into a playscript, making appropriate changes and sometimes adding details to make the playscript easier for actors to use.[1]	Works together effectively and independently on a role-play, portraying characters and also adding own ideas.

Writing[1] Give learners another short diary extract or a story from the Student's Book and let them change this into a playscript.

Speaking and listening[1] Let learners try different characters. This could help them build confidence if they find another character easier to role-play.

Unit 8 • Putting on a show

Week 3

Key strands and substrands: Lesson outcomes

Reading
- Order words alphabetically
- Use own lists of interesting words and dictionaries

Writing
- Plan and write a playscript
- Use appropriate features and layout
- Express a viewpoint in fiction
- Evaluate own and others' work

Speaking and listening
- Use non-verbal techniques, show awareness of audience
- Listen, respond, ask and answer questions
- Portray character through speech, gesture and movement
- Evaluate own and other's talk
- Discuss how meaning can be expressed non-verbally

Resources
- Student's Book pages 95–96
- Workbook page 52

Introduction

This week, learners will write their own playscript about an issue or dilemma, using what they have learned about playscript structure.

The Student's Book contains some prompts and ideas for possible topics, though if you prefer you could substitute ideas that are more appropriate for your particular class. Depending on the needs of your learners, you may decide to give them a topic to write about yourself rather than giving them a free choice. Alternatively, you could ask them to create a playscript version of part of a novel they have recently read.

Support: Learners could be asked to write a playscript version of the role-play they undertook in Week 2, based on *Zlata's Diary*. The role-play work will give them a head-start in understanding the characters and they will already have ideas about how the different characters would react.

Whatever approach you take, it is important to give learners the opportunity to rehearse their scenes out loud in a group before they write them down.

This writing exercise can be used as an end of unit review opportunity.

Student's Book pages 95–96

Writing

Ask learners to follow the prompts in the Student's Book as they plan their dialogues. They could work in groups, in pairs or individually. (Group working is helpful, especially for learners who are struggling,

since the whole group can role-play and support each other in writing the same story.) Encourage plenty of discussion, and prompt learners to practise telling their story to a partner before they begin writing.

Learners will need to think carefully about their dialogues and plan how to include descriptions as well as interesting speeches, so it may take them more than one session to write a complete draft. It's therefore helpful to allow plenty of time for the planning and drafting stages.

The prompts in the Student's Book can be used as a checklist to remind learners of the key elements they should be checking at draft stage. If time allows, the groups could perform their plays to the rest of the class at draft stage in order to get additional feedback before making a final version.

It is helpful to either watch or read the plays yourself at draft stage too, so that you can comment and steer the groups to write a successful final draft.

When all the plays are complete, give the groups an opportunity to act them out – perhaps to parents, or to other classes in an assembly.

Workbook page 52

Vocabulary (continued)

2 Some learners may benefit from completing the Workbook activity on alphabetical order during this writing exercise. This activity is helpful in reminding learners how to look up unknown words in a dictionary – which is something they may well need

Unit 8 • Putting on a show

to do as part of checking their work. The definitions below are examples, so accept other accurate definitions.

Answers
2

Word: alligator	Definition: a large reptile a bit like a crocodile
Word: anger	Definition: an unpleasant feeling of rage and unfairness
Word: angrily	Definition: in an angry way
Word: balance	Definition: put something in a steady position so it doesn't fall
Word: bath	Definition: a tub you can fill with water and lie down in to wash
Word: beetle	Definition: an insect with hard wing cases
Word: brim	Definition: the very top edge of something
Word: fairground	Definition: a place where fairs take place
Word: flying	Definition: travelling through the air

Word: seahorse	Definition: a small fish that lives in the sea and looks a bit like a horse
Word: seaside	Definition: the land next to the sea
Word: submarine	Definition: a vehicle that can travel underwater
Word: subtle	Definition: not very obvious or showy
Word: trainers	Definition: sports shoes
Word: triangle	Definition: a shape with three sides
Word: triple	Definition: three times, or having three parts
Word: valiant	Definition: brave
Word: valuable	Definition: worth a lot of money

Student's Book page 96

Thinking time

Allow time for learners to reflect on what they have learned about dealing with difficult problems from the diary and play in this unit.

Weekly review

Use this rubric to assess learners' progress as they work through the activities this week. You can use the activities suggested beneath the table to follow up on your on-going assessment.

Level	Writing	Speaking and listening
■	Can write a simple playscript when working within a clear structure.[1] Can include some simple stage directions as well as speech.	Needs support to listen and respond appropriately to others when role-playing and when acting from a playscript.
●	Can work more independently, and may be able to come up with their own scenario for their playscript. Can include stage directions where necessary. Playscript may or may not resolve the dilemma they are writing about.	Can normally listen and respond in a group when role-playing or acting from a playscript. Listens to other's work and ideas and sometimes gives helpful advice.
▲	Can write a longer and more complex playscript, including powerful verbs and adverbs (especially in the stage directions). Can work independently and are able to come up with ideas for improving and extending their playscript.[2]	Can work independently, listening and responding to others' ideas appropriately and giving advice. Listens and responds appropriately when role-playing or acting from a playscript.

Unit 8 • Putting on a show

Writing[1] Learners may write a short and simple playscript, perhaps based on the story that they know well. Their playscript should give a sense of the issues involved.

Writing[2] Learners can write a longer and more complex playscript, perhaps with parts for four or more characters. Encourage them to try to find a resolution to the dilemma they are writing about, within the playscript.

Unit 9 Imaginary worlds

Unit overview

This unit gives learners the opportunity to read a fantasy story set in space, and to write their own fantasy story using the five-stage structure. They will also compare and contrast two poems about imaginary creatures, and write a detailed description of a setting, as well as writing their own non-rhyming poem about a mythical creature. They will answer comprehension questions and express their own viewpoints. They will also practise their listening and speaking skills by making a presentation and acting out an alternative ending to a story, revise how to write and punctuate direct speech, and explore a range of spelling patterns. They also identify homonym pairs and learn to use meaning to help them decide which word of a pair to use.

Introducing the unit

Collect pictures of fantasy beasts and creatures from well-known texts that your learners would enjoy. Stories such as J.K. Rowling's *Fantastic Beasts* and C.S. Lewis's *Chronicles of Narnia* are good sources, as are some comic books and films about superheroes. Talk about the creatures and describe them. Talk about the fantasy worlds that writers create as settings for their stories. Some of these, the science-fiction stories, are set in imaginary worlds out in space, while others are set in imaginary worlds that are more like what we know on Earth.

Then select and read an extract from a fantasy which you think will appeal to your class. Talk about the characters and the setting. After that, play the audio recording of the introductory part of *Sheetal's First Landing* (or read it aloud to the class) twice. The text of the story is on PCM 23. If you wish, you can give learners copies of the text so they can follow it as you read.

Week 1

Key strands and substrands: Lesson outcomes

Reading

- Read and understand the features of a fantasy story
- Predict what might happen in a story
- Skim to gain an overall sense of a text
- Find explicit and implicit meanings and make inferences
- Identify viewpoint
- Identify and understand figurative language
- Explore how verb forms are used in texts
- Identify the main ideas in a story
- Describe the main stages in a story
- Describe how settings and characters are developed
- Comment on a writer's choice of words
- Describe the time and context of a story
- Record words in spelling logs

Writing

- Explore and use silent letters
- Describe a setting, choosing words, including specialised vocabulary, for impact

- Punctuate dialogue
- Use different verb forms
- Use powerful adverbs
- Write alternative beginnings and endings

Speaking and listening

- Listen and respond, asking and answering questions
- Take turns in discussion, contributing comments
- Takes roles in groups
- Portray a character using speech, gesture and movement

Resources

- Student's Book pages 97–102
- Workbook pages 53–56
- Slideshows: *Sheetal's First Landing* (introduction); *Sheetal's First Landing*
- Audio files: *Sheetal's First Landing* (introduction); *Sheetal's First Landing*
- PCM 23: *Sheetal's First Landing* (introduction)
- PCM 24: Story mountain

Unit 9 • Imaginary worlds

Student's Book page 97

Listening and speaking

1–2 Tell learners that the first time they hear the story you just want them to listen carefully and enjoy it. The second time, they should make some notes using the prompts in the Student's Book. Encourage them to use the bullet point prompts to make headings they can write under, to speed up the note-taking process.

Ask learners where this story is set (on a planet far from our world). How do they know this? Spend a few minutes looking for clues about the setting in the story. Establish that this is a fantasy story set in an imaginary world. Make links with any similar stories or films that learners may be familiar with.

3 After the second reading, allow plenty of time for learners to discuss their prediction ideas in pairs and prepare to present these to the rest of the class. Agreeing on a shared prediction may be challenging for some pairs, so support them as they discuss this and if necessary, model how to listen politely to each other and arrive at a compromise. Then give each pair a limited amount of time (perhaps two minutes) to explain what they think will happen next in the story.

You can use PCM 23 for a follow-up spelling activity. Give each pair of learners a copy of the PCM and a highlighter pen. Ask them to highlight all the words that have a long *ee* vowel sound (regardless of spelling). They can then classify the words they find into groups according to spelling pattern, and think of some other words with each spelling pattern to add to their list. You could use the lists as the basis of a classroom wall display, and learners could continue to add words that they find in their reading to the appropriate lists. The lists can then be used for spelling practice and revision.

The relevant words from the extract are:

- *ee* spelled *i*: alien, mysterious
- *ee* spelled *ee*: Sheetal, been, needed
- *ee* spelled *y*: galaxy, party, safety, very, busy, really, everything, happy, everybody, quickly, everyone, possibly
- *ee* spelled *e*: enormous, me, be, we
- *ee* spelled *ea*: leap, leader

The text also includes the word 'people', but don't focus on 'eo' as a spelling pattern because it is really unique to this word!

You can use PCM 23 to revise other spelling patterns too – for instance, learners could use it to identify and group words with other long and short vowel phonemes, words with common inflections such as *–ing* and *–ed*, words with prefixes and suffixes, homophones, and so on.

Workbook page 53

Reading and speaking

Revise common silent letters in spelling: c, b, g, k, n, w, t, u, and l. Write some examples on the board and read them aloud to the class.

Then read all the words in the box on page 53 of the Workbook aloud to the class. Let them listen carefully but don't tell them which letters are silent.

Answers

Silent c	Silent b	Silent g	Silent k	Silent n
science	doubt	sign	knight	autumn
scene	bomb	gnome	knee	column
ascend	lamb	gnat	knew	hymn
scientist	debt	foreign	knife	solemn
scenic	crumb	resign	kneel	
scent	comb	campaign	know	
scenery			knot	

Silent w	Silent t	Silent u	Silent l
wreck	bristle	guitar	calm
wrong	castle	guilty	balm
wriggle	listen	guess	walk
wrinkle	jostle	disguise	chalk
wrap	rustle	guest	talk
wreckage	thistle		half
			calf

Student's Book pages 98–100

Reading and writing

1 Learners can tackle the reading and comprehension individually or in pairs. Before they read the story in detail, let them skim it and say what they think the gist of the story is. Circulate as learners read the story, and answer any questions they may have. If there are words that they do not know, discuss the meanings and write the words and definitions on the board for future reference.

2–4 Many of the comprehension questions are open, but even for more closed questions, always allow learners their own variations in the answers, as long

Unit 9 • Imaginary worlds

as the sense of the answer is correct, and the language used is appropriate.

Check that learners understand that dialogue often uses different tenses from those in the main narrative.

Thinking deeper

Learners can read the story again and then close their eyes and imagine that they are Sheetal and they are about to make a landing in a new place. They write down the first five words that come to mind. They then arrange the words to make a poem.

The poem can have five lines of one word each, or two lines with two or three words in each line. The poem should be short and spontaneous.

Some learners may prefer to draw their own pictures to show this rather than think of words to describe their feelings.

Support: Learners could work in pairs or groups to find more sentences from the story that are in the past, present and future. They could use PCM 23 for this too, annotating it to show which tense each sentence uses.

Extension: Have learners complete the following activity to develop their understanding of how tenses are used. The dialogue in a story is often written in the present tense or the future.

- Choose two sentences of dialogue from *Sheetal's First Landing* and say them to your partner in the past tense.
- Which tense makes the story more interesting? Why do you think this?

Learners should understand that dialogue often refers to the past or future as well as the present, because the characters might be talking about things they have done in the past or are going to do in the future.

Workbook page 54

Verb tenses

1–2 Follow this up by asking learners to complete the Workbook activities on tenses in speech, either in class or for homework.

Unit 9 • Imaginary worlds

d "Kenzie <u>was</u> the winner of the running race." (past)

e "When I <u>was</u> little, my favourite toy <u>was</u> a bear." (past)

f "We <u>had/ate</u> a big chocolate cake on my birthday." (past)

g "<u>Are</u> you ready to go out?" (present)

h "Mum <u>is</u> calling you!" (present)

i "My favourite team <u>is</u> Real Madrid." (present)

Student's Book page 101

Listening and speaking

1–2 Circulate while learners discuss what might happen after the end of the story, and prepare to act it out in their groups. Help them to negotiate together so that everyone gets a chance to put their ideas forward. Give them time to rehearse their scene; the groups could then take turns to perform it for the whole class. Encourage them to use their voices and gestures to help make the scene exciting for the audience.

After all the groups have performed, talk about the different ideas. Did all the groups have different ideas, or were some of them similar?

Use the prompts in the Student's Book to introduce learners to the idea of a story mountain. Point out how it is similar to the five-stage story structure they learned about in Unit 4 (and spend a few minutes recapping this if necessary).

3 You could use the story mountain on PCM 24 to analyse *Sheetal's First Landing*. This is an interesting story to analyse because of the open ending. Point out to learners that even though the story doesn't tie up all the loose ends at the end, it still ends at a satisfying point. One way of mapping the story to the five-stage structure is:

- Introduction: Sheetal leaves the spaceship and goes down on to the planet surface.
- Build-up: she walks across to the tomb and is winched up to the roof.
- Climax: she winches down into the tomb and sees the alien mummies.
- Resolution: she attaches the sensors and returns to the ship.
- Climax: the sensors show the aliens coming alive...

While the groups discuss how well their story idea fits the structure, circulate among them so that you

can help to resolve any problems. Learners could use PCM 23 to record their ideas.

Student's Book page 102

Reading and writing

1–3 Use the Student's Book prompts to remind learners about expressive and descriptive language. You could undertake activities 1 and 2 as a whole class, and learners could then tackle activity 3 in pairs or independently.

Answers

The choice of sentences for activities 1 and 2 is partly a matter of opinion, but if you tackle these questions as a whole class there will be an opportunity to discuss the options and share reasons for a particular choice of sentence. For activity 3, accept any appropriate and grammatically structured sentences that fulfil the question requirements.

Extension: Learners should be able to revise their story to make it reflect the five-stage structure with little help or support. Encourage them to discuss the options and make sure that everyone in the group has a chance to put forward ideas.

Support: Learners may benefit from your assistance to think of ways in which their story can be made to fit the structure. Prompt them to take notes to remind them of their new story structure.

Workbook page 55

Verbs and adverbs

1–3 Learners can attempt these activities independently, either in class or as homework.

Answers

Answers to all questions are open; accept interesting and powerful verbs, adverbs and adjectives of the learner's choice, as long as they fit with the target sentences.

Workbook page 56

Punctuation

1–2 Some learners may benefit from completing these activities on punctuating direct speech during the planning process. The activities are a revision exercise but it may be helpful to remind learners of rules for punctuating direct speech.

Unit 9 • Imaginary worlds

Weekly review

Use this rubric to assess learners' progress as they work through the activities this week. You can use the activities suggested beneath the table to follow up on your on-going assessment.

Level	Reading	Writing	Speaking and listening
■	Sometimes struggles to decode unfamiliar words and may have difficulty understanding some of what they read on a first reading.	Can write simple sentences, understanding and applying some spelling rules. Usually remembers to add final punctuation to sentences.[1]	Needs support to organise ideas and use language appropriately when discussing and agreeing ideas and acting out a story.
●	Usually reads accurately and fluently. Generally shows good basic understanding, but may need support to read more unfamiliar or challenging texts.[1]	Can write in clear sentences, normally using basic sentence punctuation accurately. Knows some spelling rules and can apply them when prompted, and sometimes independently.[2]	Uses some appropriate language, tone and gesture when acting out a story, but sometimes needs reminding to keep the tone consistent.
▲	Reads with accuracy and fluency, and able to use inference effectively to help them understand what they have read.	Can write in clear sentences and has a good understanding of basic punctuation. Knows and consistently applies a range of spelling rules.	Demonstrates good simple acting ability, usually with appropriate use of language, tone and gesture.

Reading[1] Give learners copies of PCM 23 again and let them read the story aloud in pairs to build confidence as they will be familiar with the story.

Writing[1] Learners can complete page 56 in the Workbook to practise punctuation

Writing[2] Let learners write the story of *Sheetal's First Landing* in their own words. You could give them a frame to get them started. They should only write the main ideas. Let them focus on spelling and punctuation when they check their sentences.

Unit 9 • Imaginary worlds

Week 2

Introduction

Explain that learners are going to read some poems with fantasy settings and characters.

You could use the reading activity as an opportunity to explore the differences between reading silently to oneself and reading aloud. Ask learners what they think the main differences might be, and share ideas about this. For example:

- In silent reading, you can jump forwards and backwards in the text if you need to, for example if you want to reread something in order to correct your understanding of the text.
- In reading aloud, you have to read continuously without jumping about in the text, or you may confuse your audience!
- In silent reading, the sounds of the words are relatively unimportant – you don't have to think about them much if you don't want to.
- In reading aloud, the sounds of the words matter a lot, and you need to make sure that you 'perform' the text for the listener to help them understand and enjoy it.

Student's Book page 103

Reading

As learners read the poems aloud in their pairs, circulate so you can check their understanding and answer any questions. Praise examples of good expression and intonation.

If there is time, you may want to ask the pairs to choose their favourite poem of the two to learn by heart and perform.

Student's Book page 104

Comprehension

Learners answer the questions.

After learners have completed the comprehension exercise, share their answers to question part **k** about similarities and differences between the poems.

Extension: Challenge learners to discuss the poems as a group and see if they can think of at least one additional similarity or difference to add to the ones they found.

Support: Learners may need help to articulate the similarities and differences. You could use the suggested answers to question part **k** above as the basis of a discussion with them.

> *Answers*
>
> **a** *The Last Dragon* is set near a cave, in a forest, at dusk, with snow falling. Phrases that help convey this are: 'dusk-damp cave', 'first snow falls', 'he turns his face to the winter moon', 'the first owl swoops to the forest floor'.
>
> **b** Learners should understand that the phrase suggests the setting is getting dark, damp and chilly.

© HarperCollins*Publishers* 2021

Unit 9 • Imaginary worlds

c They nest by his feet. Because he doesn't roar or breathe fire any more.

d Open question; accept any two pairs of rhyming words.

e Verse 4 uses the half-rhyme 'moon/gone' rather than a full rhyme.

f 'furled' means drawn in, closed or curled up.

g Accept any reasonable expression of feeling and ideas for what the learner would say to the dragon.

h He finds a unicorn horn.

i 'but there are no unicorns now.' Open question about why the poet repeated this line; for example, learners may think it helps to show that the poem is about things that are different now compared with in the past, or it gives a sad/wistful feeling.

j Accept any reasonable answer in keeping with the poem.

k Ways in which the poems are similar include that they are both about magical/imaginary creatures, they both have a sad feeling, they both suggest that something magical has ended or is ending. Ways in which the poems differ include that one rhymes and the other doesn't; one includes repetition and the other doesn't; the language in *The Last Dragon* is more literary and expressive; *Lost Magic* mostly uses speech-like language.

l Accept any preference that includes at least two reasons.

Thinking deeper

Some learners may be able to tackle the 'Thinking deeper' activity independently, but you could discuss it as a whole class. The question about whether the unicorns represent something else is an open one – there are no right or wrong answers and different opinions may be equally valid. One interpretation of the poem is that the unicorns might represent childhood memories – the narrator is remembering a time when he could roam freely without danger, and the world seems different now. Another reading might be that the unicorns represent friends.

Student's Book page 105

Reading and writing

1–5 Introduce the activity using the prompts in the Student's Book. If necessary, remind learners about the different uses of verbs, adverbs and adjectives before they tackle the activity.

You could do the initial, note-making part of the activity as a whole class, if you wish – this gives the opportunity to check learners' understanding of these different parts of speech, and also to make sure they understand the difference between a 'boring' or ordinary verb, and so on, and a powerful one. Encourage learners to use words from their own spelling logs and from dictionaries and thesauruses.

This writing activity shouldn't take long; depending on how difficult learners find it, they may or may not need to go through a drafting stage. Encourage them to draw pictures of the setting to go with their descriptions. When they have finished, compare the descriptions and pictures. You may be surprised how many different interpretations there are in one class!

Student's Book page 106

Reading

1–5 You could tackle this activity as a whole class, identifying the rhyming words in the poem and using these as a basis for lists of words with similar spelling patterns. The procedure described in the Student's Book can of course be used for words with any spelling pattern, so you could extend it to include words with patterns you are currently focusing on in class.

Answers
1 fall/all; old/cold; roar/more; floor/more
2 fall, all; old, cold; roar; more; floor

Workbook pages 57–58

Writing

1–6 If time allows, you can follow this up with a poetry-writing exercise. Ask learners to choose their favourite of the two poems and use it as a model for their own poem about an imaginary animal. Encourage them to reread their model poem and think carefully about how they are going to structure their own poems.

Support: Learners could be directed to write a non-rhyming poem, and use the Workbook poetry writing activity to help structure this. The Workbook activity takes learners through the planning phase of writing the poem in some detail.

Unit 9 • Imaginary worlds

Weekly review

Use this rubric to assess learners' progress as they work through the activities this week. You can use the activities suggested beneath the table to follow up on your on-going assessment.

Level	Reading	Writing	Speaking and listening
■	Needs support to understand and read a poem.	Needs extra structure and support when completing an unfamiliar writing task.	Needs support to read aloud effectively and share ideas in the group.
●	Can read an unfamiliar poem and understand the main ideas.	Can tackle a description of a setting or a poem based on an existing structure. Needs to be reminded to think about expressive language choices and apply poetic features consistently.	Can work on an oral performance of a poem, making some changes to improve their reading as necessary. Can share ideas in their group with some prompting and support.
▲	Can read a poem with understanding.	Can write a detailed description of a setting, adding extra detail to information from the text. Can write a poem independently using a clear model.[1]	Can perform a poem effectively, assessing their own reading and changing it as necessary. Can share ideas independently in their group.

Writing[1] Challenge learners to add figurative and descriptive language to their poems to create a mysterious atmosphere for the reader.

Week 3

Key strands and substrands: Lesson outcomes

Reading

- Recognise homophones and near homophones on sight
- Explore and understand punctuation of direct speech

Writing

- Plan and write a fantasy story
- Write a simple playscript
- Develop imaginative descriptions of settings and characters

- Make notes to inform writing
- Evaluate own and others' writing
- Spell homophones correctly

Resources

- Student's Book pages 107–108
- Workbook pages 59–60
- PCM 11: The structure of a story
- PCM 24: Story mountain

Introduction

For the main writing activity, learners will write their own story about imaginary worlds, following the five-stage story structure they have been taught. There are several ways of tackling this, depending on the amount of support your class needs.

The story-writing exercise can be used as an end of unit review opportunity.

The prompt pictures in the Student's Book are intended to be helpful if learners don't have specific ideas of their own about the kind of fantasy setting and creatures they would like to write about. If

individual learners have good ideas of their own that don't fit with the prompts, encourage them to use their own ideas.

Student's Book pages 107–108

Writing

Step 1: Planning

Ask learners to follow the prompts in the Student's Book as they plan their story. They could work in groups, in pairs or individually. Encourage plenty of discussion, and prompt learners to practise telling their story to a partner before they begin writing.

Unit 9 • Imaginary worlds

Support learners as they work on structuring their stories. They could use PCM 24 (or PCM 11) to help them collect ideas for their first draft. If necessary, model this note-taking and drafting process for them.

Learners will need to think carefully about their stories and factor in how they are going to include expressive language, dialogue, and so on, so it may take them more than one session to write a complete draft. It's therefore helpful to allow plenty of time for the planning and drafting stages.

Workbook pages 59–60

Homophones

1–3 These activities will extend and consolidate learners' ability to recognise and use homophones correctly. They can also be undertaken either in class or as homework, now or at any point in this unit.

> *Answers*
> **1 a** I have something in my <u>eye.</u>
> **b** My dad says my brother has a <u>hole</u> in his stomach. He ate the <u>whole</u> cake.
> **c** Have you met Yuki and Jen? <u>They're</u> from Japan and this is <u>their</u> house.
> **d** We waited at the station <u>for</u> two hours, from <u>four</u> o'clock until six o'clock.
> **e** Look at all of ships out at <u>sea</u> today. How many can you <u>see?</u>
> **f** There are <u>too</u> many cars on the road and they all seem to be going <u>to</u> the same place.
> **2** eye/I, bear/bare, by/buy, deer/dear, four/for, hour/our, whole/hole, male/mail, won/one, right/write, see/sea, sum/some, their/there, too/two, where/wear
> **3 a** <u>Where</u> are you going?
> **b** I left my bag over <u>there.</u>

> **c** Lara can <u>write</u> very neatly.
> **d** Our team <u>won</u> the obstacle race.
> **e** We've got chicken noodle soup <u>for</u> dinner.
> **f** The postman has just delivered the <u>mail.</u>
> **g** Would you like <u>some</u> juice?
> **h** The little boat was floating on the <u>sea.</u>
> **i** I finished reading the <u>whole</u> book in one day.
> **j** I went to the park and Ahmed came <u>too.</u>

Student's Book page 108

Writing (continued)

Step 2: Redrafting and revising

The prompts in the Student's Book can be used as a checklist to remind learners of the key elements they should be checking at draft stage. After an initial read-through of their own stories, encourage learners to swap stories with a partner and comment (positively!) on each other's work.

It is worth reading learners' stories yourself at draft stage too, if possible, so that you can also make suggestions.

After the redrafting stage, give learners the opportunity to write a full draft of their piece, including pictures if they wish. You could make a class book or display of the finished stories.

Extension: Learners should be able to write a longer and more complex story, using expressive language confidently to describe setting and characters, and writing appropriate and accurately punctuated dialogue.

Support: Learners may write a shorter story. Learners who struggle to write a whole story could complete the Workbook activity on alternative story openings and endings for end of unit review instead.

Weekly review

Level	Reading	Speaking and listening
■	Needs support to understand and follow the five-stage structure when writing their own fantasy story based on a model.	Needs support to listen and respond appropriately to others' ideas in discussion.
●	Can write a fantasy story, following the five-stage structure and including some dialogue and description of setting and characters, with occasional support.	Can normally listen and respond to others' ideas appropriately, with minimal support.
▲	Can write a more extended story with accuracy and fluency, following the five-stage structure and including appropriate description and dialogue, with minimal support.	Can work independently, listening and responding to others' ideas appropriately.

Unit 9 • Imaginary worlds

Task sheet 3

For consolidation and reinforcement, and to assess learners' understanding of the main learning objectives in Units 7, 8 and 9, have learners complete Task sheet 3. Mark and record the task as part of your on-going assessment. See page 6 Assessment in Primary English for guidance.

Marking guidance

Question 1

Reading

A Outside a school, in the evening. Learners should circle the bracketed section in italics under 'Scene 1: Outside school'. (2 marks, one for identifying the setting and one for circling the correct part of the text.)

B Any three from: dialogue is set out without speech marks in a play; the speakers' names go in the margin; stage directions tell the actors what to do/how to speak their lines; all the description is in the stage directions; playscripts don't tell you what people think, just what they do and say – or similar ideas in the learner's own words. (3 marks – one for each correctly identified feature.)

C Because he is unlocking his bike; One of the children: 'I thought all you children had gone home by now!' (2 marks, one for correct answer and one for correct quotation.)

D Any two from: cautiously, impatiently, urgently, thoughtfully, eagerly. Adverbs are used in stage directions to tell the actors how to move or say their words. (2 marks – half for each correct adverb, and one for correct summary of why adverbs are used.)

E He thinks Mr Harvey is a great peacemaker who can sort out a problem on his home planet. (1)

F Look for at least two speeches from each character, correctly set out and punctuated, and in keeping with the scenario described. (4 marks – one for each correctly-written speech.)

Question 2

Grammar, punctuation and spelling

A Speeches should be correctly set out as direct speech, for example: (4)
"Hmm," said Mr Harvey. "It's the big match this evening. If you promise to get me back home before it starts, I suppose I could come and see what I can do."

"Thank you, sir! Thank you!" said the alien. "Come with me: I promise you will be home before you know it."
Accept variations in wording as long as they are appropriate.
(4 marks – one mark for changing the words appropriately for direct speech in each example, and one for putting speech marks in the correct places in each example. Do not penalise the learner for misplacing final punctuation, e.g. putting it outside speech marks.)

B
Was this some kind of prank?
I came in peace, from Planet Warthog!
This was why we needed you, sir!
It could travel great distances in the blink of an eye.
(Or It travelled great distances ...)
(4 marks – one for each correctly rewritten sentence.)

C
We had a great day last Saturday.
I amazed Mum by doing all the washing up.
There is only one piece of cake left.
Dad gave me a big lump of cheese to grate.
The opposite of war is peace.
Some people like getting up early, but others don't.
I went to the shop because I wanted to buy a packet of crisps.
I've nearly finished my Maths homework, but I'm stuck on a difficult sum.

(4 marks – half a mark for each correct use of a homophone.)

Question 3

Writing

A 10 marks – award 1 mark for each of three accurately written paragraphs, and one mark for each of the following features:

- a description of the setting
- some dialogue set out as direct speech
- some powerful verbs
- some interesting adjectives
- a beginning
- a middle
- an end.

Punctuate the story

1 The text below is from a historical story, but most of the punctuation is missing. Read the story carefully. Then add the missing punctuation marks.

It was a freezing night on the streets of London and Jim and his little sister Martha were trying to get to sleep They only had a thin blanket two old coats and a few sheets of newspaper to keep out the cold Their stomachs were rumbling loudly because they hadn't eaten a scrap of food since that morning

Are you asleep Jim Martha asked I'm hungry

I'm hungry too muttered Jim. But we've got no food left so we'll just have to hope we can find some tomorrow

Just then the children heard a very unwelcome noise A policeman was coming round the corner towards them

Hey he shouted What are you two doing here

The children looked at each other It was too late to run What could they do

2 What do you think will happen next? Write another paragraph to continue the story. Remember to include punctuation.

_____

_____

_____

_____

_____

_____

_____

_____

Extract from a diary

**Read the diary entry below.
Then answer the questions.**

14 November 1867

Dear Diary,

Today is a great day for the poor child workers who have been suffering in British factories, farms and workshops.

Until recently, children as young as five years old had been forced to work in terrible conditions for almost no money. However, I am happy today because new laws have just been passed which will help to improve their lives.

From now on, no child under eight years of age will be allowed to work in any factory or workshop. In addition, children aged between eight and thirteen will be entitled to ten hours' education per week.

Campaigners like Lord Shaftesbury have been trying to bring about this change for a long time. They will be as delighted as I am with the new laws, which will protect children's health and make sure that they receive some basic education. Not everyone agrees. My ex-friend, Mr Granger, told me this morning: "It is important for poor children to work and help their families by bringing in a wage. We do not need new laws to protect children – we should be encouraging more children to work!"

I shall not be visiting Mr Granger again until he rethinks his attitude!

Ebenezer Grimes

❶ What is the main point in the first paragraph?

_____

_____

_____

_____

_____

2 **Underline the diary features below.**

- the date
- the writer's name
- the greeting
- a sentence in the present tense
- an opinion from the writer

3 **What are the main changes for working children as a result of the new laws?**

_____

_____

4 **What is the youngest age at which a child could work in a factory under the new laws?**

_____

5 **Find the phrases 'entitled to' and 'in addition' in the text. Draw circles round them and explain what each phrase means in this text.**

a entitled to: _____

b in addition: _____

6 **Do you agree with Mr Grimes's opinion or Mr Granger's opinion? Explain your answer.**

_____

_____

_____

_____

_____

_____

_____

_____

_____

_____

Diary entry

Use the writing frame below to help you write a diary entry about something that has happened recently. Remember to check your spelling and punctuation.

←— Date

←— Opening

←— First paragraph that says what happened and how you felt about it

←— Second paragraph with more detail

←— Last paragraph – explaining how you feel and what you will do next

←— Your name

Notes for a historical story

Discuss your story ideas in your group or pair. Then use the planning frame below to make some notes about the story you are going to write.

Where the story is set

When the story is set

Details to help show the reader what things were like at that time

Who the characters are and what they are like

How the story will start

Problems the characters will have

How the story will end

Paragraph plan for a story

Use the paragraph plan below to make some more detailed notes about the characters, setting and the main events in your story. Remember – this plan is just for **notes**.

Paragraph 1: introducing the characters and setting

Paragraph 2: a problem that the characters have

Paragraph 3: the characters try to solve the problem, but something goes wrong

Paragraph 4: the characters manage to solve the problem

Paragraph 5: rounding off the story with a satisfying ending

Persuasive writing checklist

1 **Below are some of the main features of persuasive writing. Look out for these features when you are reading advertisements and persuasive arguments. Be careful though – not all persuasive writing has all of these features.**

- questions addressed to the reader (for example: 'Do you like chocolate? Then you'll **love** new Wonderbars!')

- language that stirs up the reader's emotions (for example: 'Millions of helpless puppies are cruelly mistreated every year!' or 'Enjoy the happy, zingy taste of Mintios – you deserve it!')

- alliterative language where lots of words start with the same letter (for example: 'deeply delicious doughnuts')

- rhyming language (for example 'Don't delay – start today!')

- language that asks the reader to do something (for example: 'Hurry – sign up now or miss the chance of a lifetime!' or 'Write to the government and demand action!')

- lots of exclamation marks

- words that are big and bold or in different colours

- pictures and headings to break up the text

2 **Find some good examples of persuasive writing and copy or stick them here. Use another sheet if you run out of space.**

Using commas

We use commas in three main ways.

1 To separate the items in a list, for example:

● My best friends are Chang, Jack, Noah and Emily.

We don't normally put a comma before the 'and' in a list.

2 When we are writing down the words someone said, for example:

● "Wait there a moment," said Mr Edwards, "and I'll call Ella."

● "I hope it's chips for lunch," said Zac.

3 To separate the words and phrases in a sentence to help the reader understand, for example:

● Cross the road, go past the cinema, turn left by the cafe and the park is on your right.

1 **Add the missing commas to the sentences below.**

a Jack's bike has blue handlebars red mudguards a black seat and a purple frame.

b Ever since our first day at school Jack Emily Chang Noah and I have been best friends.

c "I have four pets" said Noah "and I like helping to look after them."

d "My pets are a rabbit a goldfish a stick insect and a gerbil" said Noah.

e Charlie zoomed down the stairs ran out through the front door and rushed to the playground.

f The monster's favourite foods were snail kebabs wasp sandwiches creepy crisps and jellyfish ice cream.

g "Come and have your dinner at once" said Mum "or it will get cold."

Descriptive words and phrases

Use the chart below to help you write a poem. Fill in the chart with descriptive words and phrases that show what you would see, hear, feel, taste and smell.

What can you see?	
What can you hear?	
What can you feel?	
What can you taste and/or smell?	
How does the picture or music make you feel?	

Word families

Use the diagram below to show word families. Write the root word in the box at the centre. Then write as many related words in each bubble around it. You can add more if you want to.

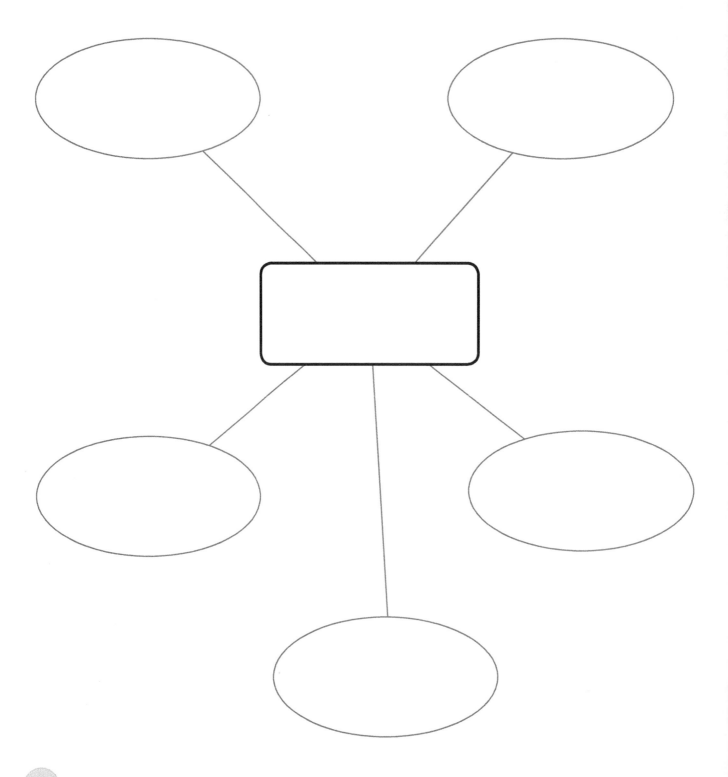

The Clever Farmer

A story from Eritrea

Once there was a farmer who had fallen on hard times. His fields were full of dust and stones, his watermelons were all shrivelled up, and worst of all, he had had to get rid of all his cows. All except one, that is. The farmer couldn't bear to part with his last cow. She was the sweetest-natured animal you ever saw, and her name was Shikorina. As long as there was a bite of food in the house, the farmer shared it with Shikorina, and they managed to get by, somehow.

But the sad day came when there *wasn't* a bite of food in the house – not even one! What was the farmer to do? He scratched his head. "I'm sorry, Shikorina my old beauty," he said. "We can't live on air. I'll have to take you to market. Perhaps I can find a rich man to buy you. He'll look after you better than I can. And with the money I get from selling you, I can buy myself a few chickens and goats, and start again."

The farmer's heart was as heavy and empty as his old iron cooking pot. He led Shikorina sadly down the road and into town.

When they got to the market-place, the farmer spotted the richest man in the district, chatting and laughing with his friends. "Good morning, sir!" said the farmer respectfully. "Can I interest you in buying this fine cow?"

The rich man looked Shikorina over carefully. "This is a decent-looking animal," he said. "She's a bit on the thin side, but aren't we all, these days? How much do you want for her, Farmer?"

"Shikorina is no ordinary cow," said the farmer. "I won't accept less than fifty gold coins."

The rich man burst out laughing. "Fifty gold coins?" he snorted. "What kind of fool are you, Farmer? No cow is worth that price! I'll give you five gold coins – take it or leave it." And the rich man turned his back on the farmer and went back to chatting with his friends.

Well, that made the farmer angry. What gave the rich man the right to disrespect him like that? "I'm not a fool!" he shouted. "No fool knows where the centre of the world is, or how many stars there are in the sky!"

The rich man wasn't used to people talking back to him, so he got angry too. "How can a poor farmer like you know where the centre of the world is, or how many stars in the sky? I'll tell you what – I'll do you a deal. If you can answer those questions, then I'll buy your mangy old cow for *sixty* gold coins!"

The rich man's friends thought this was hilarious. They slapped the rich man on the back and guffawed with laughter. But the farmer just smiled. He lifted his wooden walking-stick and plunged it deep into the ground. "There you are," he said. "This is the centre of the world. And anyone who can prove me wrong can say so now."

There was silence. No one could prove that the farmer was wrong.

Then the farmer bent down and picked up a handful of dust. "The number of stars in the sky," he said, "is as uncountable as the number of dust grains in my hand. And anyone who can prove me wrong can say so now."

Once again there was silence. At last the rich man spoke. "You may be poor, Farmer," he said, "but I can see you are rich in cleverness! I certainly can't prove you are wrong. Since I made a promise in front of witnesses, I must keep it. Here – take your sixty gold coins, and give me your cow. She will take pride of place in my herd!"

So the farmer got his money, and Shikorina got a fine new home. And the farmer bought himself some excellent goats and chickens, and within a year, he had made enough money to buy Shikorina back from the rich man – for *seventy* gold coins!

The structure of a story

Many stories follow the structure below. You can use this chart to help you work out how a story you have read fits the structure or you can use it to help you plan a story of your own.

Stage	What happens
Introduction	Sets up the story and introduces main character and setting.
Problem/Build-up	Something starts to happen. It could be a problem or something the main character has to do. Other characters may come into the story.
Climax/Conflict	The most exciting part of the story. The problem reaches a climax and there may be some conflict between the characters.
Resolution	Something happens to solve the problem.
Conclusion	Loose ends are tied up and the story reaches a satisfying ending.

The Selkie Wife

A story from Scotland

One night a selkie decided to take off her sealskin and dance on the sand. As soon as she stepped out of the sealskin she became a beautiful young woman. A young fisherman saw her and fell in love with her at once. He brought her back to his house and asked her to marry him. So that she could never leave him and go back to the sea, he stole her sealskin and hid it from her, telling her that it was lost.

The selkie was very sad because she knew that her true home was in the sea and she longed to return to it. But without her sealskin she could never go back.

The years went by and the selkie fell in love with the fisherman. They had three fine young sons and the selkie almost forgot her old home in the sea ... Almost, but not quite.

Although she loved her family she was never completely happy because she still yearned to return to the sea.

One day the selkie decided to mend some old fishing nets. She looked in the shed for a length of rope and what should she find on the top shelf but ... her old sealskin! At last she could go back home! That evening she bundled the sealskin under her arm and ran off down to the beach without telling her family.

At suppertime they realised that she had gone. The fisherman guessed what must have happened and he and his sons rushed down to the sand just in time to see the selkie slip into the waves, wearing her sealskin.

The boys and their father looked at each other sadly. They would miss her so much – but as they looked at the seal swimming away towards the horizon they knew that at least now she was happy.

119

Reading aloud

Use the checklist below to help you perform a poem or story out loud.

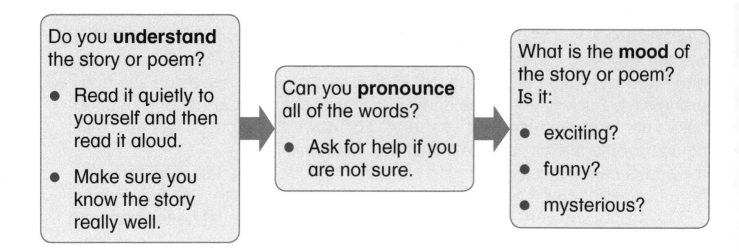

Do you **understand** the story or poem?

- Read it quietly to yourself and then read it aloud.

- Make sure you know the story really well.

Can you **pronounce** all of the words?

- Ask for help if you are not sure.

What is the **mood** of the story or poem? Is it:

- exciting?

- funny?

- mysterious?

Now think about how you can make your reading interesting.

- Can you vary the speed and loudness?

- Can you use facial expressions to show what the characters are thinking?

Practise reading your story or poem until you feel really confident.

- Enjoy your performance!

Write your own poem

Plan and write a poem about your least favourite food.

1 Think about the type of food you like least. Write its name below.

_____

2 Write some interesting adjectives to describe the food.

3 Write at least three adverbs to describe how you would eat the food.

4 Now write some stronger verbs you could use instead of eat, for example *munch*, *guzzle*, *chomp* ... How many more can you think of?

5 Think of a good line you could repeat in your poem, for example:

Mum said, "Eat your beans, eat your beans …
Just eat them!"

Write your repeating line here.

_____

_____

6 Write a draft of your poem.

7 Read your draft out loud to someone and make any changes to improve your poem.

8 Write your final draft in your best handwriting. Draw a picture to go with it.

Who, what, when, where, why?

Most newspaper articles try to answer these questions:

- **Who** is the article about?
- **What** happened? **What** did they do?
- **When** did it happen?
- **Where** did it happen?
- **Why** or **how** did it happen?

Read the newspaper article below. Then write the words or phrases that answer each question.

Who: _____

What: _____

When: _____

Where: _____

Why or how: _____

An alien? Fat chance!

Fishermen dragged a mystery 6-metre-long object with six tentacles onto a beach in Tasmania yesterday. At first it was believed to be an alien – but on closer inspection it turned out to be just a piece of whale blubber washed up by a recent severe storm.

Non-chronological reports

Use the planning frame below to write a non-chronological report.

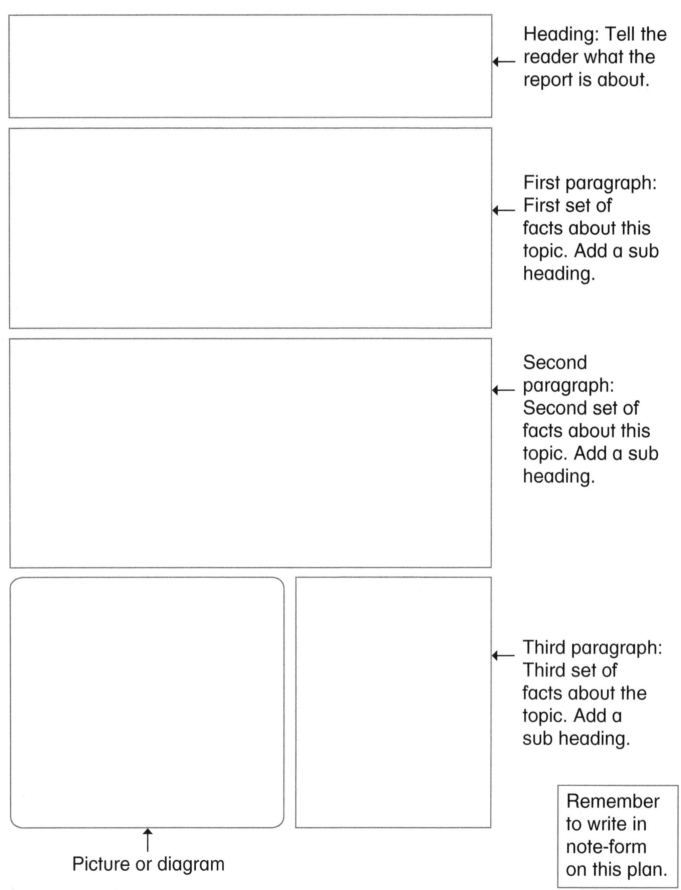

Heading: Tell the reader what the report is about.

First paragraph: First set of facts about this topic. Add a sub heading.

Second paragraph: Second set of facts about this topic. Add a sub heading.

Third paragraph: Third set of facts about the topic. Add a sub heading.

Picture or diagram

Remember to write in note-form on this plan.

Instructions

Use the planning frame below to write instructions.

Heading: Tell the reader what the instructions are about.

What you need:

-
-
-
-
-

Use bullets in this section.

What you do:

1.

Number the instructions in this section. Most of the sentences should be orders (for example, 'Cut the paper,' and so on).

Letter to a newspaper

Read the letter to a newspaper below. Then answer the questions on page 44 of the Workbook.

11 Ocean View Drive
Parklands
Cape Town

6 January

Dear Sir or Madam

I believe that the most important invention created in the last hundred years is the internet. It is hard to believe how much our lives have changed since the internet was invented. Here are just some of the ways in which the internet has improved life for most people.

First of all, the internet connects people. Families who live far apart can use video calls, so that they can see each other when they speak. People can also use email to stay in touch easily, even when there is a great distance between them.

Secondly, the internet has search engines which can help you find information in a few seconds. There are many different search engines which offer all sorts of information and suggestions. In addition, the internet is a brilliant source of entertainment. Whatever your interest you will find something to enjoy on the internet.

In conclusion, I believe that the internet is the best invention of the last century. I would certainly not like to go back to life before the internet was invented.

Yours faithfully,

A Baxter

A. Baxter

Writing a friendly letter

Use the writing frame below to help you write a letter to a friend.

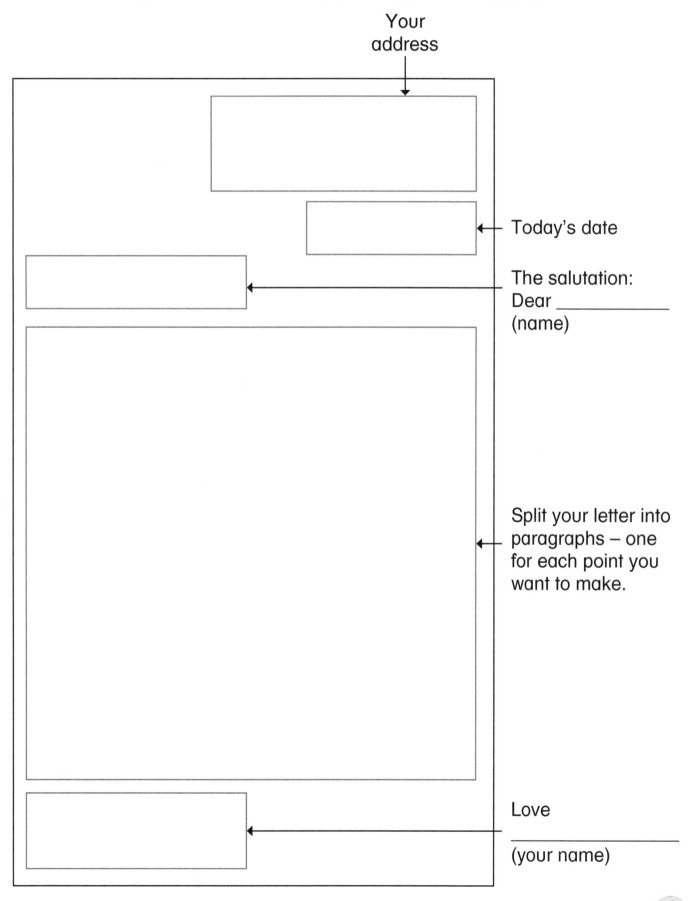

Your address

Today's date

The salutation:
Dear _____
(name)

Split your letter into
paragraphs – one
for each point you
want to make.

Love

_____
(your name)

Writing a formal letter

Use the writing frame below to help you write a formal letter.

Your address

The address of the person or business to whom you are writing.

Today's date

Salutation: Dear Sir or Dear Madam

Split your letter into paragraphs – one for each point you want to make.

Yours faithfully

_____ (name)

Peter and the Wolf: story summary

Peter lived with his grandfather in a cottage in the middle of a forest. In front of the cottage was a green meadow but Grandfather wouldn't let Peter play there. He kept warning Peter that a wolf was out there in the forest waiting to gobble Peter up.

Peter wouldn't listen to Grandfather. He loved playing in the meadow because his friends Duck and Bird lived there. Peter's Cat loved the meadow too – especially when he was trying to catch Bird!

One day Grandfather caught Peter in the meadow playing with Duck, Cat and Bird. Grandfather was very angry and sent Peter straight to his room.

As soon as Peter and Grandfather had gone the wolf came out of the forest and tried to catch Cat! Just in time, Cat leapt up a tree. Then the wolf decided to eat Duck instead – and after a long chase he caught her! He snapped her up in one gulp.

Luckily Peter had seen what happened. He climbed out of his bedroom window and fetched a rope. Then he crept over to the tree where Bird and Cat were sitting. The wolf was at the bottom of the tree snapping and trying to catch Bird and Cat. They were trapped!
Peter climbed up the tree without the wolf seeing him. He told Bird to fly around the wolf's head and make him dizzy. Then Peter made his rope into a lasso and caught the wolf's tail. He hoisted the wolf up into the tree and tied the rope round a branch so the wolf was trapped.

Just then a hunter came along. He wanted to shoot Bird – but when Peter explained that he and Bird had just caught the wolf, the hunter changed his mind! He agreed to help Peter and his friends take the wolf to the zoo where he wouldn't cause any more trouble.

Grandfather was very proud of Peter when he realised how brave he had been. So everyone was happy ... or nearly everyone! Duck was still trapped inside the wolf's belly. He had swallowed her whole!

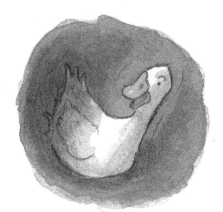

A difficult decision: character cards

Use the cards below to help you get into role and decide what your character would say.

Zlata

You quite like mice! You think it's funny that after all the work everyone did, the mouse has come back again. You find this funny but know you have to get rid of the mouse because Mummy is so scared of it.

Daddy

You are very fed up when the mouse comes back! You worked all morning to get rid of it and now it's here again! You feel quite cross about it.

Mummy

You are really worried and upset about the mouse. You just want to run away from it – but you also feel a bit silly for being so scared.

Sheetal's First Landing: introduction

Sheetal has grown up on a huge spaceship that explores the galaxy. Now her help is needed to investigate a mysterious alien planet.

This was it! My first ever landing! I'd spent all the nine years of my life so far on our enormous expedition spaceship; I'd never really been outside, only on training simulations. I paused just a second at the hatch of the spaceship, getting my suit cameras to record everything. Then I stepped down, onto the planet surface, where five people in space suits were waiting. "One small step, one giant leap!" said the Landing Party Leader. That's tradition – it's what the Leader always says when someone steps onto their first planet. The Leader stuck a "Landing Party" badge on my space suit, and saluted. Then she added "Happy birthday, Sheetal." Everybody clapped and whooped. I was so excited – but I told myself to be calm and professional. The expedition had no time today for anyone messing up, or showing off, or causing problems.

We needed to finish our work on this planet quickly, because an enormous, dangerous storm was coming. So everyone who could possibly help was needed. Our main job here was to explore a mysterious alien tomb. The landing party needed a small, agile person who could get inside the tomb and put sensors there. I could do that – I had passed my tests on sensors and on planet safety yesterday.

It was the very best ninth birthday I could imagine! No birthday cake, and no presents for me today: we were all far too busy for that. But really – who cares about cake or presents if you get to go *outside*?

Story mountain

Use the story mountain template below to help you plan a story.

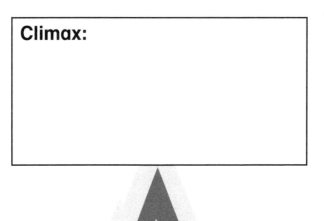

Climax:

Build-up:

Resolution:

Introduction:

Conclusion:

Task sheet 1: Units 1–3

Read the poem at least twice before you answer the questions.

The bicycle's wrists

You must grip them carefully,
both at the same time
as though you were leading

a partner onto the dance floor

long slender arms extended
into the blue air of the street,
with just a touch of stiffness
as though neither of you were
sure of the steps.

So you wobble then move
on an impulse forwards
you and the wrists
hanging on for dear life

as if dancing were all
that kept you from falling.

by George Szirtes

Question 1

Reading

A What do you think the bicycle's 'wrists' are? (1)

B What other sort of activity does the writer compare riding a bicycle with? (1)

C Write two phrases that show the person in the poem is not confident about riding a bike. (2)

D Imagine you are watching the scene described in the poem. Describe the scene in your own words. (2)

_____

_____

E How does this poem make you feel? Explain your reasons. (2)

_____

_____

Question 2

Spelling, grammar and punctuation

A Find four verbs in the poem that end in the suffix –*ing*. (2)

_____   _____

_____   _____

B Add the suffix –*ing* to these root verbs from the poem. Think about whether you need to change the spelling of the root verb when you add the suffix. (2)

grip   _____

extend   _____

wobble   _____

keep   _____

C Find two connectives in the poem. (1)

_____

D Read the first verse of the poem below. Write it out as if it were a sentence of direct speech. Add all the correct punctuation. (2)

> You must grip them carefully,
>
> both at the same time
>
> as though you were leading
>
> a partner onto the dance floor

_____

_____

_____

E Write adjectives from the box below that have a similar meaning. (2)

nervous	world-beating	terrified	good

a frightened   _____   _____

b excellent   _____   _____

Question 3

Writing

A Read this description of an invention. Draw a wavy line under all the opinions and a straight line under all the facts. (4)

- This is the world's most amazing bicycle.

- It's ideal for nervous cyclists and people who are just learning to ride.

- It has a lightweight titanium frame and chunky puncture-proof tyres.

- It comes in a range of colours including black, silver, turquoise, orange and flame-red.

- It can be used on every type of surface – including roads, fields, mountains and even sandy beaches.

- It is every cyclist's dream.

- It stops automatically if the rider is in danger.

- If you fall off or crash the bike's built-in crash pads activate automatically and catch you.

B **Write a persuasive advertisement for this invention. (5)**

- Give the invention a name.

- Use facts, opinions and persuasive language.

- Use the information in part A and add your own ideas.

- Write at least five sentences.

_____

_____

_____

_____

Task sheet 2: Units 4–6

Read the newspaper article below. Then answer the questions.

One giant leap

Have you ever wondered what it would be like to jump from 39 kilometres above the surface of the Earth? Ask Felix Baumgartner – the only human being who has ever tried it.

Ever since he was a boy Felix has dreamed of flying. He did his first skydive (jumping out of an aeroplane with a parachute) at the age of 16 and he has never looked back! Felix has clocked up many daring feats and world records in his career. For example, he holds the world record for the highest BASE jump from a building. In 2007 he jumped with a parachute from the top of the 509-metre high Taipei 101 building. But for Felix the ultimate challenge was to annihilate Colonel Joe Kittinger's record for the highest ever skydive. Kittinger set the bar high – literally – when he skydived in 1960 from a height of 31 kilometres. So when Felix came to try to beat the record he enlisted Kittinger's help to ensure he got everything right. The adventurous duo worked with a team of experts to ensure that Felix had all of the equipment and training he needed to make a safe jump from the astonishing height of 39 kilometres above Earth. Felix even needed a specially designed protective pod to take him to the site of the jump, right on the edge of space.

After many months of preparation the great day finally came. At 9.28 a.m. on 14 October 2012 Felix's pod was attached to a huge helium-filled balloon that slowly lifted him all the way up to the jump point. Two and a half hours later, at 12.06 p.m., Felix jumped. Less than a minute after evacuating the pod he had reached his maximum speed of 1,358 kilometres per hour. That's faster than the speed of sound!

After four minutes 20 seconds of free fall Felix opened his parachute. Just nine minutes after making the jump he touched down safely in the New Mexico desert – and smashed the skydiving world record!

Question 1

Reading

A Read the first sentence of the report again. What is the purpose of using this sentence at the beginning of the report? (1)

_____

B Why did Felix Baumgartner want Joe Kittinger to help him prepare for his record-breaking skydive? (1)

_____

C How did Felix's pod reached the jump site? (1)

_____

D Write two sentences describing Felix Baumgartner. Use your own words. (2)

_____

_____

E How long did it take Felix to reach Earth on his record-breaking skydive? (1)

_____

F What record-breaking feat did Felix carry out in 2007? (1)

_____

_____

G Write one sentence to sum up the main point of this newspaper report. (1)

_____

Question 2

Grammar, vocabulary and punctuation

A Write one statement, one question and one order from the newspaper report. (3)

_____

_____

_____

B Change each sentence into an order. Write the order on the line below. (2)

Would you like to find out about the champion skydiver Felix Baumgartner?

_____

You could tell your friends about Felix's amazing adventure.

_____

C Underline the powerful verbs in these two sentences. At the end of each sentence write another verb that could be used instead of the one you underlined. (2)

For Felix the ultimate challenge was to annihilate Colonel Joe Kittinger's

record for the highest ever skydive. _____

Less than a minute after evacuating the pod he had reached his maximum

speed of 1,358 kilometres per hour. _____

D **Write the sentences below with the correct punctuation. Add a capital letter and a comma to each sentence. (2)**

Felix Baumgartner jumped from an astonishing 39 kilometres above earth a record-breaking jump.

_____

_____

Felix took a team of experts lots of equipment and a protective pod to the jump site on 12 october 2012.

_____

_____

Question 3

Writing

A **Read the description below. It is about another amazing feat by Felix Baumgartner.**

Felix wanted to try something never done before, so in 2003 he skydived all the way across the English Channel. This was very difficult because he had to glide for 36 kilometres during the free fall, in order to get across the Channel.

To do the skydive, he wore a specially designed set of wings that allowed him to glide. He looked like a human aeroplane.

Felix's English Channel skydive

Location: English Channel

Height: 9.8 kilometres

Distance travelled: 36 kilometres

Top speed: 360 kilometres per hour

Journey duration: six minutes, 22 seconds

Write a newspaper report about Felix's English Channel skydive using the information on page 140. It must include at least five sentences. (10)

Remember to include:
- a headline
- a punchy opening
- the key facts
- your own opinion of what Felix did
- at least two sentences with powerful verbs.

Task sheet 3: Units 7–9

Read the playscript below. Then answer the questions.

Mr Harvey and the Alien

SCENE 1: Outside school.

(It is evening. Only MR HARVEY, the headteacher, is still at school. He is just unlocking his bike and is keen to go home.

An ALIEN appears behind him as if from nowhere. MR HARVEY doesn't notice at first.)

ALIEN: *(cautiously)* Er ... excuse me?

MR HARVEY: *(impatiently, still bending down and unlocking his bike so he can't see the alien)* Yes? What is it? I thought all you children had gone home by now!

ALIEN: Are you the famous and powerful leader Mr Harvey?

MR HARVEY: *(straightening up, still with his back to the alien)* Ha! Well I don't think I've ever been called that before!

ALIEN: *(urgently)* We need your help sir!

MR HARVEY: *(turning around and seeing the alien)* Oh my goodness! Is this some kind of prank?

ALIEN: No sir! I come in peace from Planet Warthog! It is many light-years from your galaxy. My ship's computer has led me to you sir. It tells me that you are a great peacemaker who can bring enemies together and find solutions to terrible problems!

MR HARVEY: *(thoughtfully)* Well ... I suppose I did manage to stop that fight between Jack and Zoltan this afternoon ...

ALIEN: *(eagerly)* Exactly! This is why we need you sir! My planet is troubled with problems almost as terrible as the war between Jack and Zoltan. Only you can help us. Will you come with me? My ship is waiting. It can travel great distances in the blink of an eye.

MR HARVEY: Hmm. It's the big match this evening. If you promise to get me back home before it starts, I suppose I could come and see what I can do.

ALIEN: Thank you sir! Thank you! Come with me: I promise you will be home before you know it.

(A space ship appears in front of them. The ALIEN leads MR HARVEY inside and the space ship vanishes.)

Question 1

Reading

A i What is the setting of this playscript? (1)

_____

ii Draw a circle around the part of the playscript that gives you this information. (1)

B Give three ways playscripts are different from stories. (3)

_____

_____

_____

C i Why does it take Mr Harvey a while to realise he is speaking to an alien? (1)

_____

ii Who does he think he is speaking to? (1)

_____

D i Write two adverbs from the playscript. (1)

_____

ii What is the purpose of the adverbs? (1)

_____

E What does the alien want Mr Harvey to do? (1)

_____

F Write a new ending for the playscript. Imagine what might have happened if Mr Harvey had said no to the alien.
Write two speaking lines and stage directions for each character. (4)

_____

_____

_____

_____

_____

_____

_____

Question 2

Grammar, punctuation and spelling

A Read this conversation from the playscript. Write it out again in direct speech, as if it came from a story, not a play. Remember to add the correct punctuation and words like 'said Mr Harvey'. (4)

MR HARVEY: Hmm. It's the big match this evening. If you promise to get me back home before it starts, I suppose I could come and see what I can do.
ALIEN: Thank you, sir! Thank you! Come with me: I promise you will be home before you know it.

_____

_____

_____

_____

B The sentences below are in the present tense. Change each sentence to the past tense and write it out. (4)

Is this some kind of prank?_____

_____

I come in peace, from Planet Warthog!_____

_____

This is why we need you, sir!_____

_____

It can travel great distances in the blink of an eye._____

_____

C The following words from the playscript are homophones. Choose the correct homophone from each pair to fill the gaps in these sentences. (4)

peace/piece   by/buy   some/sum   great/grate

We had a _____ day last Saturday.

I amazed Mum _____ doing all the washing up.

There is only one _____ of cake left.

Dad gave me a big lump of cheese to _____.

The opposite of war is _____.

_____ people like getting up early but others don't.

I went to the shop because I wanted to _____ a packet of crisps.

I've nearly finished my Maths homework but I'm stuck on a difficult _____.

Question 3

Writing

A **Write a short story of at least three paragraphs. The story should be about what might happen when Mr Harvey arrives on the alien's planet. (10)**
Remember to include:

- a description of the setting
- some dialogue set out as direct speech
- some powerful verbs and interesting adjectives
- a clear beginning, middle and end.

Cambridge Global Perspectives™

Below are some examples of lessons in *Collins International Primary English Stage 4* which could be used to develop the Global Perspectives skills. The notes in italics suggest how the English activity can be made more relevant to Global Perspectives.

Please note that the examples below link specifically to the learning objectives in the Global Perspectives curriculum framework for Stage 4. However, skills development in a wider sense is embedded throughout this course and teachers are encouraged to promote research, analysis, evaluation, reflection, collaboration and communication as general best practice. For example, the pair work and group activities suggested throughout this Teacher's Guide offer opportunities to develop skills in communication and collaboration which build towards the specific Global Perspectives learning objectives.

Cambridge Global Perspectives skills	Learning Objectives for Stage 4	Collins International Primary English Stage 4
RESEARCH	Information skills • Locate relevant information and answers to questions within sources provided	• Unit 2, Week 3, Writing Step 1: SB p24, TG p37 *Provide learners with books and documents or access to websites that you know contain the required information.* • Unit 3, Week 3, Writing Step 1: SB p37, TG p46 *Provide learners with books or access to websites that you know contain the required information. Support them in focusing on relevant information as suggested in the TG.*
EVALUATION	Evaluating sources • Discuss a source, recognising that the author has a clear viewpoint on the topic	• Unit 2, Week 1, Reading and speaking: SB p16, TG p30 *Focus the discussion on the purpose of the advertisement and how the author / producer has tried to achieve that purpose.* • Unit 2, Week 2, Reading: SB p21, TG p34 *Focus the discussion on identifying the viewpoint the author is promoting.*
REFLECTION	Personal viewpoints • Talk about what has been learned during an activity and consider how personal ideas have changed	*The Thinking time sections at the end of some units give opportunities for learners to reflect on activities and what they have learned. Encourage and support them to express what they have learned and how this might have changed their ideas or learning strategies they will use in the future.* • Unit 1, Week 3, Thinking time: SB p12, TG p27 • Unit 3, Week 3, Thinking time: SB p38, TG p47 • Unit 4, Week 3, Thinking time: SB p50, TG p57 • Unit 9, Week 3, Thinking time: SB p96, TG p95

Text acknowledgements
The publishers gratefully acknowledge the permissions granted to reproduce copyright material
in the book. Every effort has been made to contact the holders of copyright material, but if
any have been inadvertently overlooked, the Publisher will be pleased to make the necessary
arrangements at the first opportunity.

Cover illustration: *The Brave Baby* Reprinted by permission of HarperCollins*Publishers* Ltd ©
2004 Malachy Doyle, illustrated by Richard Johnson.
Let's Go To Mars Reprinted by permission of HarperCollins*Publishers* Ltd © 2005 Janice Marriott,
illustrated by Mark Ruffle; *The Brave Baby* Reprinted by permission of HarperCollins*Publishers*
Ltd © 2004 Malachy Doyle, illustrated by Richard Johnson; *Peter and the Wolf* Reprinted by
permission of HarperCollins*Publishers* Ltd © 2007 Diane Redmond, illustrated by John
Bendall-Brunello.

We are grateful to the following for permission to reproduce copyright material:
Extracts on p.60 from *Goggle Eyes* by Anne Fine, Penguin, copyright © Anne Fine, 1989.
Reproduced with permission of David Higham Associates; Extracts on p.73 from 'Mini Mars
Mission', www.firstnews.co.uk Reproduced with permission of First News; Extracts on pp.99,
131 from *Sheetal's First Landing* by Chris Baker, copyright © Chris Baker, 2015. Reproduced by
kind permission of the author; Excerpts from the poem on p.102 "The Last Dragon" by Judith
Nicholls, published in *Storm's Eye*, Oxford University Press, 1994, copyright © Judith Nicholls,
1994. Reproduced by kind permission of the author; An extract on p.123 from "An Alien? Fat
Chance!", *Daily Mail*, 14/01/1998, copyright © Solo Syndication, 1998; and the poem on p.133
"The bicycle's wrists" by George Szirtes, published in *In the Land of Giants*, Salt Publishing,
2012. Reproduced by kind permission of the author.

Photo acknowledgements
The publishers wish to thank the following for permission to reproduce photographs. Every effort has been made to trace copyright holders and to obtain their permission for the use of copyright materials. The publishers will gladly receive any information enabling them to rectify any error or omission at the first opportunity.

p108 Peter Higginbottom Collection/Mary Evans Picture Library, p117 Frances Linzee Gordon/ Getty Images.